*Flights of Fancy,*
*Leaps of Faith*

# Flights of Fancy, Leaps of Faith

## CHILDREN'S MYTHS IN CONTEMPORARY AMERICA

### Cindy Dell Clark

THE UNIVERSITY OF CHICAGO PRESS
CHICAGO AND LONDON

Cindy Dell Clark is an adjunct faculty member in the Marketing
Department at DePaul University.

The University of Chicago Press, Chicago 60637
The University of Chicago Press, Ltd., London
© 1995 by The University of Chicago
All rights reserved. Published 1995
Printed in the United States of America
04 03 02 01 00 99 98 97 96 95   1 2 3 4 5

ISBN: 0-226-10777-9   (cloth)

Library of Congress Cataloging-in-Publication Data

Clark, Cindy Dell.
    Flights of fancy, leaps of faith : children's myths in
contemporary America / Cindy Dell Clark.
        p.      cm.
    Includes bibliographical references (p. 139) and index.
    1. Imagination in children.   2. Fantasy in children.   3. Tooth
loss—Psychological aspects.   4. Christmas—Psychological aspects.
5. Easter—Psychological aspects.   I. Title.
BF723.I5C55   1995                                      94-38890
                                                              CIP

Illustrations on page 89 are from *Familiar Mysteries: The Truth in
Myth*, by Shirley Park Lowry. Copyright © 1982 by Shirley Park
Lowry. Reprinted by permission of Oxford University Press, Inc.

*To Bill and Will*

# Contents

# Acknowledgments

This book owes much to the many adults and children who have inspired and taught me. They include my anonymous informants—busy Americans all—who took time out of their lives, even during holiday vacations, to share their experiences with me. Several industry researchers have helped as interviewers, and their names are included in the appendix. In addition, I'd like to thank Holly Blackford, who brought her intelligence (and holiday spirit) to helping prepare this manuscript.

Much of this research was done under the astute guidance of Richard A. Shweder. I owe a great debt to him, for his conceptual brilliance, his ability to bring the best of reason and romanticism to a problem, and his willingness to care about a student's own issues (even the Tooth Fairy). I am also grateful to my other steadfast and supportive advisors, Peggy Miller and Ray Fogelson. Jean Comaroff, Wendy Doniger, James Fernandez, Gary Alan Fine, Gil Herdt, Peter Homans, Stanley Kurtz, Melanie Wallendorf, and Rosemary Wells have all been of service, by reacting to my ideas and research in progress. And I am thankful for the fellowship grant from the Harris Center for Developmental Studies that made this work possible.

While the ideas in this book are mine, gifts of intellectual and moral support along the way have been given by generous spirits indeed. Milk and cookies are due for all.

# One

# Introduction

Nobody sees Santa Claus, but that is no sign there is
no Santa Claus. The most real things in the world are those
that neither children nor men can see. Did you ever see fairies
dancing on the lawn? Of course not, but that's no proof they are not
there. Nobody can conceive or imagine all the wonders there are
unseen and unseeable in the world.
—Francis Church, *New York Sun,* 1897

It is only with the heart that one can see rightly;
what is essential is invisible to the eye.
—Antoine de Saint Exupéry

Once upon a time in Western history, when adults and
children both believed in fairies, there was no question
but that the most essential realities were invisible to the
eye. Spiritual beings, from leprechauns to angels, were an accepted part of the plane of existence, even to grown-ups. No
more. In today's skeptical era, the hallmark of "mature reasoning"
is to be able to distinguish "fantasy" (occult things) from "reality"
(patent things).

Yet fairies and their compatriots have refused to retreat entirely
in the face of empirical skepticism. Every year at Christmastime,
American parents find that Santa Claus has descended upon their
children's world with substantial vigor. If a child loses a tooth,
the ethereal Tinker Bell–like Tooth Fairy lets her light shine upon
the household. And of course, each spring the Easter Bunny
comes hopping down the bunny trail, as invisibly and quietly as
Elwood Dowd's movie companion, Harvey.

It stands to reason that the lingering presence of such sprites
and pookas would raise some questions in the logical mind. As

ageless as Santa Claus himself is the age-old discussion of whether it is right to have children believe in him. Some parents conclude that promulgating the Santa Claus custom is like lying to their children: Jehovah's Witnesses and other fundamentalist Christians—not to mention countless secular humanist philosophers have reached such a reasoned conclusion. Philosopher Judith Boss, writing in the journal *Free Inquiry,* has maintained that free thinkers should stifle belief in Santa Claus. She has argued: "To claim that we need Santa Claus to teach children the spirit of goodness and generosity is to assume that his spirit exists only in make-believe and that it does not exist in real people and relationships."[1]

In the face of such arguments, what is a contemporary parent (or student of childhood) to conclude? Does believing in Santa Claus undermine faith, or in some paradoxical way does it serve to support faith? What about the materialism associated with customs involving vast numbers of toys (Santa Claus), vast quantities of candy (the Easter Bunny), or even cold, hard cash (the Tooth Fairy)? One nine-year-old interviewed during the research for this book referred to Santa Claus as the "god of presents": Is that all he is to children? Has Santa Claus got anything to do with the less material meaning of Christmas?

Questions like these about Santa Claus and the rest of the childhood pantheon have led to much armchair speculating by grown-ups as to whether Santa Claus is good or bad for children. Yet until now, very few of Santa's own followers—children— have been consulted in the matter.

In what follows, I present ethnographic fieldwork that goes directly to children to assess their experience firsthand. I have interviewed in depth 133 children and seventy-two mothers, most often in their homes, in some cases with help from colleagues. Other mothers kept "field notes" recording their children's behavior for the six-month period including Christmas and Easter, 1989–90. I have also analyzed videotapes of children visiting Santa and the Easter Bunny in a shopping mall. (To protect the privacy of research participants, all names have been changed. See the appendix for a more detailed discussion of the child-centered approach I have taken.) As a result of this extensive research, a rich picture of how children themselves frame and give meaning to these customs emerges. This fieldwork will help answer the questions adults ask about American childhood customs.

Without doubt (reasonable or otherwise), children have much to teach adults about matters of faith. Those of tender years are apt to "reach out to eternity" in passionate ways, as Robert Coles's recent book *The Spiritual Life of Children* documents.[2] When adults want to reach out spiritually, some find themselves wishing for childlike trust to replace their cynicism and skepticism. Those in the midst of the youthful "wonder years" occupy a life stage when awe and suspended disbelief are tolerated, even valued, in our culture. Magic dragons, unicorns, and Ninja Turtles tend toward youthful devotees.

What, then, can children teach adults about how faith is possible, and how the material-based customs and myths (Santa, the Bunny, and the Fairy) nourish or discourage faith? Does childhood ritual leave our kids and us with more than tinsel and wrappings and celluloid grass as lasting leftovers?

Insofar as childhood myths are early excursions into culturally shared *imaginal* experience, they enlighten us about the benefits and workings of such experience. Imaginal experience can be defined as that experience which is not physically present, but which is actually experienced nevertheless. One finds imaginal experience across the life span and in different contexts: conversations with a doll or special teddy bear (what D. W. Winnicott has called the transitional object) or with a companion such as Harvey or Hobbes (in the cartoon strip *Calvin and Hobbes*); and in dreams, prayer, or fantasy. Such experience is called imaginal (rather than imaginary) since one cannot presume to label it as ultimately subjective or objective. The reality of these phenomena is sustained by the active participation of the experiencer's imagination, but they are not judged to be unreal. As Winnicott has argued about transitional phenomena, imaginal phenomena occupy a paradoxical space which is neither within the individual nor outside in the world of shared reality.[3] Imaginal phenomena depend upon faith. As J. M. Barrie, originator of the dramatic character Peter Pan, has written,

You see children know such a lot now, they soon don't believe
in fairies, and every time a child says "I don't believe in fairies"
there is a fairy somewhere that falls down dead.[4]

To the extent that fairies require the faith of children in order to
be experienced, they are special beings not to be labeled as either
fantasy or reality. Rather, they serve to draw from and strengthen
the imaginal capacity.

In reading this book, you are invited to remember (as Paul
Veyne has reminded) that one is most at ease in studying beliefs
when one realizes that truth is plural.[5] Children experience the
world in ways that differ from adults, but their experience has
just as much validity and their faith just as much truth and sacredness as the faith and experience of adults. Children's sacred beliefs
should hardly be belittled as untrue or as cute fantasy. Youthful
beliefs form the developmental foundation for imaginal experience and for awe-inspired faith. What a pity if adults have forgotten so much along the way that we can envision childhood make-
believe only with condescension, and no longer with any measure
of awe and appreciation.

# Two

# Flight toward Maturity:
## *The Tooth Fairy*

Somehow she knew at once that he was Peter
Pan. . . . He was a lovely boy, clad in skeleton leaves
and the juices that ooze out of trees, but the most
entrancing thing about him was that he had all his first teeth.
—J. M. Barrie, *Peter Pan*

Blessed is the Tooth Fairy. . . . What a comfort it is to have a
mysterious friend who compensates you, tooth by tooth, for the lost
tokens of your childhood. This special companion ignores normal
holidays and seasons, and appears only at the moments dictated
by your own body.
—Morrie Warshawski, *Parenting Magazine*

All I want for Christmas is my two front teeth, / So I
can wish you Merry Chrithmath.
—Don Gardner

## MAGICAL HEALING TO THE RESCUE

A better informant could not have been found to tell us about the contemporary American Tooth Fairy than Jimmy, a seven-and-a-half-year-old middle-class boy of Italian-Irish extraction living on Chicago's northwest side. Jimmy had lost his front tooth (the sixth baby tooth—or as they say, "milk tooth"—he had lost) about two weeks before I interviewed him at home one autumn day. Jimmy's mother alerted me to the situation. This last tooth was wiggling for a couple of weeks, and he wanted it out in the worst way. It was bothering Jimmy. Then one morning, getting ready to leave for school, he was in the back bathroom brushing his teeth. His mother called to him to come so she could brush his hair. All of a sudden she heard a scream, then tears and crying. He had been brushing his teeth when the bothersome tooth had fallen out and gone down the bathroom drain.

Jimmy's tears didn't surprise his mother:

> He couldn't leave his tooth for the Tooth Fairy if he didn't have the tooth. . . . And I said, "It's OK, Jimmy, I'll call Uncle Joe . . . and maybe he could take the sink apart and get the tooth." I wasn't really going to ask him to take the sink apart, but he had to get to school. And then I told him that night that "they couldn't get it apart. But it happened to a friend of ours, when they did take it apart, they couldn't find the tooth anyway. But maybe if you left a letter for the Tooth Fairy." So he did and taped it to the front door.

Taping the note to the front door (for the Tooth Fairy to see as she "flies by") seemed to do the trick. "She gave me the money and everything," Jimmy explained to me—and he still had the dollar squirreled away in a drawer. What Jimmy didn't know was that his mother had saved the note he wrote and had tucked it in her wallet along with her mercenary "valuables." Penned in Jimmy's own printing, the note read:

> Dear The Tooth Fairy,
> Sorry the tooth can't come because I was brushing my teeth and it fell down the drain.
> Love, Jimmy

Jimmy was sure that the Tooth Fairy is a she, as most children I've interviewed would agree, even though he had not personally seen her. With exceptional imagination, Jimmy speculated that the Fairy might live in "some dentist's office," hiding somewhere unbeknownst to the dentist. ("If she's an inch small like I think she is, she'd be in a drawer somewhere.") It was no coincidence that the Fairy was associated, in Jimmy's mind, with a dentist: Her job has to do with the trauma of losing a tooth and children's fear of toothlessness.

CDC: If you were going to talk to somebody like your little brother, and they never lost a tooth before and they didn't know anything at all about the Tooth Fairy, what would you tell them about it?

JIMMY: I might tell them that when you lose your tooth, you put it under the pillow. The next morning you'll get something for it. And not to worry because you'll get another tooth. You won't be toothless after you lose all your teeth.

CDC: It's important to know you're not going to be toothless, a kid should know that part?

JIMMY (nodding): The tooth they lost, I think they'll understand it better and not think it'll hurt or anything.

CDC: You think kids think it might hurt?

JIMMY (nodding): The fairy godmother, if they never saw the tooth, I think they might [think that].

CDC: What if the Tooth Fairy stopped coming? What if the Tooth Fairy said, "I'm tired of doing this. . . . I'm not going to come any more when kids lose their teeth? How would that be?"

JIMMY: I'd just glue the tooth back into my mouth. I'd leave it glued. And you don't really deserve any money for it, just a tooth.

CDC: What's more important, getting the money or getting another tooth?

JIMMY: Getting another tooth.

From a child's perspective, the Tooth Fairy is a way to handle the *loss* of the tooth—far more than many parents realize. This aspect is foregrounded in Jimmy's case because Jimmy had experienced a double loss: losing the already lost tooth down the bathroom drain. In turn, Jimmy's transaction with the Tooth Fairy centers on loss: "Sorry the tooth can't come because I was brushing my teeth and it fell down the drain" is Jimmy's explicit message to the Tooth Fairy. "Sorry you lost your tooth, but you'll get another one, and here's some money in the meantime" is the Tooth Fairy's implicit message to Jimmy.

So important is the easing of this loss that Jimmy guesses that God himself gave the Tooth Fairy her job.

CDC: How did the Tooth Fairy get started doing this, do you suppose?

JIMMY: Probably God made them. . . . One day Adam or Eve, either one, lost their tooth, and didn't know what to do with it. So God spoke to them, and she told them, put your tooth when you're sleeping and it'll go away and you'll get something for it.

CDC: How come God knew they'd need to do that? . . . How do you think he thought they'd feel?

JIMMY: He figured, toothless! Then they might not be able to bite so well.

CDC: So God made the Tooth Fairy and said, put the tooth under your pillow, and that's that? What did the Tooth Fairy think about getting the job?

JIMMY: Happy, . . . because not too many people get to see God while they're living, and then the Tooth Fairy got to see him any time that she wanted to, if she had any questions or anything. And she was a very special person because people wouldn't want to be toothless.

Spiritual intervention to reassure kids that tooth loss won't hurt and won't be permanent is warranted, as far as Jimmy is concerned. His case is not exceptional. Children described to me a host of physical displeasures that can accompany losing a tooth. There is bleeding and discomfort when too much pressure is applied to the loose tooth, as when eating or when someone pulls a tooth. There is the potential of swallowing the tooth, which happened to a few young unfortunates. And there can be difficulty in talking. (The lisp lampooned in the song "All I Want for Christmas Is My Two Front Teeth" is indeed a reality for some kids; by some cruel mistiming of speech development, many kids begin to make sounds such as "th" just when they lose the teeth needed to make these sounds.) Children are enthusiastic about getting "big teeth" or "grown-up teeth," but there's certainly need for a lot of reassurance along the way.

Being reassured about losing one's teeth is undoubtedly a deep human need. In literature (including biblical literature) and folklore, teeth have long been characterized as representing potency, beauty, and pain. A terrible Old Testament curse was to appeal to God to break the teeth of one's enemies. Toothlessness is a state associated with helpless dependency, exemplified in infants and the elderly. Such expressions as "arming ourselves to the teeth," "fighting tooth and nail," and "escaping by the skin of our teeth" reveal the risk to power that the loss of teeth represents.[1]

Dreams of losing teeth are widely reported among adults, as Freud and others have noted, not only in Western culture but around the world. During an interview, one mother reported with a white-faced look of shock and fear a recent dream: She had dreamt of all her bottom teeth coming out, one by one. Years earlier, she dreamed she was appearing on the Johnny Carson show as the teeth fell out of her mouth and everyone stared.

Although both dreams frightened her deeply, this woman attached no particular significance to either. But many people do think that tooth-loss dreams are meaningful. In other cultures from central Africa to Mexico, dreaming of losing a tooth has been widely interpreted as portending the death of a relative or near friend.[2] Western psychoanalysts have interpreted such dreams as representing varied concerns: fears of castration or of growing old, desires to return to infantile dependency—even personality disintegration.[3] In *The Interpretation of Dreams,* Freud associated tooth-loss dreams with masturbation.[4]

That tooth loss is such a rich metaphor for loss, retreat from power, and vulnerability would not surprise youngsters. Children experiencing second dentition, firsthand, make it clear how upsetting the experience can be. At times, I've been told, losing a tooth can be worse than getting stitches, or worse than getting allergy shots. The loose tooth is aggravating and "bothers you." It hurts when you eat or brush your teeth. The bleeding is "icky" and "disgusting"—sending some tooth losers into a near panic. Especially for the first tooth, one is apt to be scared: The required courage is itself enough to make you into a "big girl," a girl named Sarah told me. And the concern that one might remain toothless, as Jimmy described, is a serious matter to some children. After all, one uses teeth to chew and eat and thereby survive. Kids losing their first tooth can worry that they "won't have no teeth," in the words of one first-grade girl, and "won't be able to eat."

If there is enchantment in the Tooth Fairy ritual, it partly comes from its power to allay these concerns through the transformative meaning of expressive symbolism, turning second dentition into a positive, valued experience. Consider the story told by Peter, age seven, whose father took it upon himself to yank out the child's tooth personally (as it is not atypical for control-minded fathers to do).

> When we were at our grandmas for a sleepover, [my dad] said, "Come here," and he yanked it out. It hurted pretty much. . . . I didn't know what he was gonna do. Finally, he just reaches into my mouth and yanks it out, and I'm [shrieking noise]. I'm screaming and I go, "OOOOOWWWWWW." And I said, "Did you do it to me?" and he goes, "Yeah." And he shows me that [tooth]. And I didn't feel the pain 'cause I started jumping up and down and saying, "Yeah! I'm gonna get the money!"

Jennifer (age eight), explaining why she thought the existence of the Tooth Fairy is a "good idea," also testified to an attitudinal shift provoked by the ritual.

> Sometimes when you're a little kid, I know when I was five, when I heard I was gonna lose my teeth, I said, "Well, am I ever gonna get it back? What's gonna happen to me? Will I be toothless for the rest of my life?" And so I sort of got a little scared. And I think that it was a good idea because when you lose it, then you get something in return. And you'll get a new one that's better.

The Tooth Fairy is largely a Western custom, having evolved in the cultural melting pot of the United States, most likely during the nineteenth century.[5] But all over the world, shed-tooth rituals of varied forms have eased this process for children. Anthropologists and dental folklorists report a remarkable array of such customs, whereby the lost deciduous tooth is discarded in some meaningful way.[6] For example, the tooth might be buried with an ancestor (New Guinea), in the hearth or fire (Sheffield, England, ca. 1895), or at the entrance to the lodge (Teton); left for a squirrel (Bohemia) or beaver (Cherokee) or some other straight-toothed animal; blackened with charcoal (Chippewa); or tossed into a mouse's hole (Mexico) or into the sea for a many-toothed dolphin (Patagonia). Often, some kind of incantation is spoken aloud when the tooth is placed. In Vietnamese society, children toss the tooth over the roof of the house (if an upper tooth) or onto the ground (if a lower tooth), calling out to the rats: "Oh rats! Oh rats! Since your teeth are both long and pointed, you must work in such a way that mine shall grow as quickly as they fall out." A Cherokee child recites, "Beaver, put a new tooth into my jaw." Among the New Zealand Maori, a song is sung:

> Sprouting seed, sprout
> Sprout that you might come
> To see the full moon
> Come you sprouting seed
> Let the teeth of the man
> Be given to the rat
> And those of the rat
> Be given to the man.

A particularly exotic form of shed-tooth ritual occurs among the Wendish population of Spreewald: The parents are supposed to swallow their child's tooth—mother swallowing a son's, father swallowing a daughter's (parental control indeed!).

With striking regularity, the developmental process is aided by external powers (such as ancestors or potent animals), who are called upon to give good, straight teeth. Often this involves what anthropologists term "sympathetic magic"—calling upon an object with the necessary qualities (say a rodent with strong, prominent teeth) to impart these qualities to the needy party. (Presumably, dentistry, with its X-ray magic, reduces the worry about good, straight replacement teeth in our culture, since dentistry itself explains the process, to adults at least.)

Yet even with modern medicine, a child's body image needs to accommodate the loss of a body part, be it tonsils removed through surgery, hair cut off by the barber, or natural loss of teeth.[7] To come to terms with losing "a part of you," it is therapeutic—even cathartic—that the baby tooth be purposefully put to rest, rather than tossed off at random. The analogy to a funeral runs deep, in that the tooth is entrusted to a higher, supernatural domain (the realm of the Tooth Fairy) as a kind of final resting place.

The grief involved in coping with loss, whether loss of a loved one or of a body part, needs to be expressed. Ritual provides a way to work through the separation and to discharge fear and apprehension about a new status.[8] Even children sense the analogy to a funeral: When thinking about offering a tooth to the Tooth Fairy, Lisa was reminded of her backyard burial of a dead goldfish (buried ceremonially—and perhaps too appropriately—in the empty matchbox from a seafood restaurant).

Just as a corpse is placed in a casket prior to burial, a tooth is commonly placed in a special receptacle, a Tooth Fairy pouch, to wait for the Tooth Fairy's exchange. Such Tooth Fairy pouches are a fairly recent innovation, thought to be invented by Elizabeth Bryant of Winter Park, Florida, in 1974,[9] but since then widely copied. A Tooth Fairy pouch is usually a handcrafted item, either crocheted, embroidered, or hand sewn. (My son has a wooden box bought at a church crafts fair, shaped and hand painted to look like a tooth.) Tooth pillows or pouches are commonly made for the child by a relative or perhaps purchased from the individual women who make them at crafts fairs. Often, a relative or friend gives a Tooth Fairy pouch to a child as a gift, before the child loses any baby teeth. Such a gift has the social effect of endorsing the Tooth Fairy custom and encouraging that the healing ritual be observed.

## FEMININITY AND FAIRIES

Jimmy imagined the Tooth Fairy to be a miniature female, and this was a common perception in the imaginal experience of children. When asked to draw the Tooth Fairy, children drew pastel-colored female figures, often with wings or wands.

Cultural symbols tend to have systematic, interrelated meaning. Pastels are colors we associate with being female (or a baby). Fairies are female, not male: Who has ever heard of a fairy godfather? Intriguingly, the popular use of the word *fairy* to refer to a male homosexual has been used to satirize the Tooth Fairy in cartoons in dental journals, as if to underscore that she is actually female. By taking on a feminine gender, the Tooth Fairy identifies herself as belonging to the realm of home, domesticity, mothers, and early childhood (as opposed to the more mature, literate male world outside the home).

In her therapeutic, healing role, the Tooth Fairy deals with tooth-shedding children in a mode more feminine than masculine. There are ancient precedents for differing approaches to healing among female as opposed to male healers. Dental hygienists, typically female, take their name and their approach to health from the goddess Hygeia, who represented health as an ongoing, natural process of living wisely. By contrast, the male god Aesculapius represented engineered intervention in illness. Dentistry is more like Aesculapius, rational and oriented toward intervention—akin to fathers who pull out kids' teeth. Yet even within the ancient male-medical cult of Aesculapius, there were female members to whom one could pray for cure.[10] These female beings represented nurturance, warmth, concern, intuitive understanding, and relatedness, the very qualities children ascribe to the Tooth Fairy.

## A RITE OF PASSAGE

As a part of the body, the baby tooth is symbolic not only of lost power and vulnerability, but of early childhood itself. For children, giving up their first teeth is symbolic of relinquishing early childhood and getting "big teeth" (so that, as one girl said, "no one can call you a baby"). How fitting, then, that Peter Pan—the mythical boy who never grew up—never gave up his baby teeth (and thereby avoided growing older).

Mothers are well aware that losing one's baby teeth constitutes a rite of passage, a milestone along the course of growing up. In interviews mothers drew comparisons between second dentition and other life transitions important in contemporary America: learning to walk or to ride a two-wheel bike, kindergarten, puberty, Roman Catholic First Communion, getting a driver's license, and so on. Explaining what the Tooth Fairy custom represents to her, Mrs. Smith replied:

> A rite of passage [laughter]. I don't know what better words
> to say to you. I don't know whatever words would fit it, except

every kid loses their teeth in order to get their new teeth to grow up. So, it's a rite of passage.

Time and again, mothers said that tooth loss is a public, tangible sign that their child was "growing up," "getting older," and entering a stage of greater independence ("he's leaving us," "getting independent"). The change in a child's physical appearance during second dentition makes it hard for a mother to ignore her child's increasing maturity. As Mrs. Brown put it:

> If you look at someone and they're missing a tooth, [they] look really different. Or say a child who loses two at once in the front, and they start lisping. It just changes their way of talking, their looks. And when their baby teeth go and their adult teeth come in, it changes their whole look. . . . I used to try to picture my kids with adult teeth, with secondary teeth. [I'd think,] This kid is so cute right now. How in the world can he be any cuter with secondary teeth? Isn't that a weird thing to think? But I did. I used to look at their pictures from kindergarten and think, oh, I wish they could stay like this. I wish their little teeth could stay. . . . You don't have a choice in losing teeth. It happens. No one can get around it.

Second dentition, in American society, occurs simultaneously with the child's transition from home to formal education, associated with a host of other changes, such as learning to read and write, that indeed serve to make a boy or girl more independent of home and more socially and cognitively skilled within the public domain outside the home. Getting grown-up teeth signals that a child is ready for this major shift in arenas. Kindergarten and first-grade teachers often keep charts in their classrooms that mark the occasion when children lose teeth, treated as a cause for celebration. One educational researcher has gone so far as to suggest that second dentition should be used to judge school readiness, since it correlates well with other measures of readiness.[11]

Tooth loss, then, is a natural symbol of shedding one developmental stage and entering another. This is not unique to American society. Across cultures, it is common for children in the five-to-seven-year age range to shift social status and expectations with second dentition. The Ngoni of Malawi, in central Africa, believe that "children who [have] lost their first teeth, and acquired their second, [have] reached a new stage in their development." When Ngoni children complete second dentition, they are held accountable for discourtesy, they are recognized as "ready for a different kind of life," and boys change places of residency.[12]

Tooth loss constitutes, quite literally, the kind of transition Arnold Van Gennep considered in his now classic work, *The Rites of Passage*. Van Gennep's great insight was to notice that rituals of passage tend to work via three stages: (1) leaving the status or role one had prior to the transition (such as when a bride is "given away" by her father); (2) entering an ambiguous middle ground, in which the person is no longer what he or she was yet has not taken on a new status either (a bride wears a veil partly to symbolize this ambiguity of being "betwixt and between"); and (3) consummating the passage when the new status is acquired.[13]

When a child loses a tooth in contemporary American culture, among the Ngoni, or elsewhere, these three stages are *literally* expressed. First, the loss of a deciduous tooth naturally *separates* the child from babyhood (just as ceremonies of mutilation accompany the separation phase of many initiation rites). Second, the child enters a naturally produced period of *ambiguity*—toothlessness—that embodies (quite literally) the "invisible" qualities often associated with the transition phase. (Jokes and humorous teasing are common at this ambiguous stage—called by dentists and some mothers the "ugly duckling" phase.) Third, the natural eruption of the secondary tooth quite literally *incorporates* in the child grown-up qualities. The three-part rite of passage is literally carried out as a bodily code in second dentition.

Van Gennep's three-step model in life crisis rituals is also found in the American Tooth Fairy custom on another level, the single Tooth Fairy visit: (1) The child *leaves* their tooth under the pillow to be *taken away* by a fairy (a Tinker Bell–like symbol of early childhood); (2) The child then goes to sleep amid dreamlike darkness (which gives effective invisibility and ambiguity); (3) The child awakens to find a gift of money (a symbol of the worldly, adult domain of grown-up people).

Because the Tooth Fairy visits repeatedly as successive teeth are lost, the actual sequence is not definitive and closed in its impact. (In this respect, the Tooth Fairy custom may differ from shed-tooth rituals in other cultures, where it is common to ritually discard only the *first* lost tooth.) Children lose teeth, one by one, over a period of years—in effect, an extended period of being betwixt and between, what dentists call "mixed dentition."

The child's belief in the Tooth Fairy also goes through a period of being betwixt and between, as children begin to doubt the Tooth Fairy as a separate figure and perhaps try to stay awake at night to catch the real fairy in the act. At this stage children are apt to vacillate between rational certainty and hopeful belief. One boy who completely discounted the Tooth Fairy's reality regained his faith entirely when he had to have two teeth pulled. The developmental process is fraught with paradox, reversal, and gradual change.

But eventually the child stops believing in the Tooth Fairy, once and for all. The emergence of disbelief is itself said by mothers to be a rite of passage. As Mrs. Martin expressed it:

> Anytime you have a kid that still believes in something magical, it still makes you feel that they're still little. Because as soon as they stop believing in all that stuff, and they're not involved in all the fun stuff that you do when you're a little kid, and then you finally realize that, OK, they figured it out, they're smart enough now, it's another stepping stone.

Once children become disenchanted with the Tooth Fairy, they have, in effect, embraced adult-defined reality. The quintessential accusation of adult naïveté is the oft-heard comment "If you believe that, I bet you still believe in the Tooth Fairy." The Tooth Fairy metaphorically provides a kind of reality check, a check to see if one is living in a "childish, fairy-tale" world, or in a "rational, mature" world.

Typically, American mothers are not eager to break the bonds of their child's tender dependency. The maternal hope, rather, is to slow the rate of separation from their child, to make sure that he/she "doesn't grow up too fast." One mother, whose son had started kindergarten the week of my interview with her, became tearful when discussing her son's lost babyhood. Mothers certainly want their children to feel "special" when they lose a tooth. But they are not anxious for their children to stop believing in the Tooth Fairy, signaling the end of childhood in a fuller sense than losing a tooth. During interviews, mothers nervously double-checked that young believers were out of earshot before explaining, in whispered tones, their deceptive role in acting out the ritual. Mrs. Adams spoke of her warning to older siblings—to "break your neck then and there"—if they told their younger brother there was no Tooth Fairy.

According to mothers' reasoning, the harsh reality of (adult) society is held at bay as long as the childish world of make-believe (Santa Claus, the Easter Bunny, and the Tooth Fairy) is maintained. Mrs. O'Connor, explaining why she wished *she* could still be a child, said that, as a child, "I wouldn't have to worry about anything [because] as a kid, it always seems like it's such a make-believe world. Then you grow up and there's reality." This sentiment was echoed in Mrs. Green's comment.

> I would love him to believe in Santa for long. I want him to believe in everything. I want Danny to believe the whole world's fine, everything's wonderful, and all these great things happen to little kids. . . . I think it's very important that they just let their imagination go and go and go. Because eventually they're going to get older and they're going to realize, and that'll be it.

Maintaining a child's belief gives the mother some force toward extending childhood: Having a role as the Tooth Fairy vividly ensures that the child is "underneath my wings" (to quote the words of Mrs. White):

> I'm still known as Tooth Fairy. . . . it's kind of, I've kept them children—even though they do go and get on their bicycles and they ride down the block and see a friend. This is the one thing that keeps them underneath my wings, and I still have them in protection. . . . Even though they think, "I'm old, and my two-wheel bike, and I can cross the alley," . . . yet there's part, they are kids yet. 'Cause they still believe that. I think I

might, the day I have to explain about Santa and the Tooth Fairy, I think I'll be a little crushed. Because it's almost like a magic spell I've broken a part of, another sign of growing up, when this [ends,] the fairy tale, the imagination. 'Cause you want to cushion your kids. And you'd love to think you can cushion them all their life.

Out of thirty-two mothers interviewed about the Tooth Fairy, twenty-two kept their child's shed primary tooth/teeth after collecting them. The tooth was said to serve as a memento or reminder of the child's babyhood. Often, these dental keepsakes were put in a location signifying special value, such as the mother's jewelry box, a baby book, or, as with Jimmy's note, a wallet. Like bronzed baby shoes, a child's christening dress, or trimmings from a child's first haircut (or even, as true for one mother, a saved pacifier), the retained teeth were valued tokens of their child's first life stage. As best illustrated by their own comments, mothers hesitate to relinquish that first life stage completely.

They just change so quickly, you can't hold on to it. But you can hold on to their teeth or a lock of their hair or something like that.

Sometimes I stop and look at them [the teeth in my jewelry box] and sort of, I'll notice them, and I'll stop. And it's always amazing to me that they're so tiny. I suppose that's what I notice about them if I stop to notice them. Because, you know, adult teeth are really quite large. And these things are just teeny-weeny, teeny-weeny little teeth. Of course, they were teeny-weenier people, too. My older one is almost thirteen, so she thinks she's grown up.

In essence, the Tooth Fairy ritual provides the American mother with symbolic "reverse gears" that decelerate the process of recognizing their son's or daughter's new age status. By saving the child's primary teeth until feeling ready to discard them and by steadfastly protecting her child's belief in the Tooth Fairy (so much so that telling a child the truth is taboo), the mother makes the child seem, in maternal perception, less grown up.

But what about the child's perspective on the ritual? It is the *growth-enhancing* meaning brought by the Tooth Fairy that motivates children to gladly undergo the discomforts of tooth loss. Children feel that their teeth are put to rest by the Tooth Fairy in a suitably reverent manner: deposited in her ethereal home, which, like heaven, is "up there," in the sky, far away. Many youngsters imagine that the Fairy uses the teeth to make something valuable—jewelry, flowers, even stars. One child thought that she gives the tooth to a new baby, recycling it.

And children feel that the Tooth Fairy gives them fair compensation, in the form of money, for their shed teeth. Money is a grown-up, empowering entity. In American society, money is a symbolic means to obtain power and independence. No doubt money is made all the more culturally attractive by its early association with the awe-inspiring, supernatural Tooth Fairy: Several young informants felt that the monetary gift was manufactured by the Tooth Fairy with the aid of her magic wand.

Children perceive having money as a way to "buy whatever I want," to have buying power that is not dependent on parental benefactors. Six-year-old Carson said that, after the Tooth Fairy's visit, "I feel like I am a new person. . . . I feel like I'm seven"—partly due to the fact that "I lost lots of teeth," but also because "When you get older you get money." Eight-year-old Jan told the story of saving her Tooth Fairy money in order to treat her mother and sister to a snack at McDonald's—a gesture that led her to observe, "I like carrying around my own money. I feel more grown up and special." When their supply of Tooth Fairy money was kept at home, children were prone to run and fetch their stash of cash and to finger through it, Scrooge-like, while showing it to me. Several children had bank accounts in which to "save for college"—the ultimate training ground for adulthood. Clearly, the possession of money makes children feel independent (since independently wealthy) and empowered. The money received from the Tooth Fairy is a valued treasure connoting a degree of autonomy, escalating the child's sense that they are older, more grown up. The icons of maturity within the Tooth Fairy ritual are plural: The child gets adult teeth, but also gets money as a symbol of being grown up.

Writing encodes another form of maturity: literacy. Written correspondence between the child and the Tooth Fairy is a common occurrence. Letter writing typically begins out of necessity, such as when the child misplaces the lost tooth (as with Jimmy) or wants to ask the Tooth Fairy if they can keep the tooth. Occasionally, the correspondence starts at the mother's/Tooth Fairy's initiative ("Congratulations on losing your first tooth," or "Keep brushing your teeth"). A few young informants had decided to carry on extensive exchange of notes with the Tooth Fairy, so as to question her about certain facts ("Do you look like the picture in the book we have about you? [   ] Yes [   ] No"). In two families, this note writing became so extensive that the Tooth Fairy impersonator developed her own signature and handwriting (in very tiny letters) to use in replies. Ironically, as mothers used correspondence to encourage their daughter's or son's belief, all the while children were getting practice in the grown-up skills of reading and writing.

Here, then, is the paradoxical dynamic of the Tooth Fairy ritual, which makes it an apt (yet subtly complex) family rite. Some symbolic elements within this rite of passage, the money, the acquired secondary tooth, and—where applicable—the note writing, serve as accelerators that make a child feel older. Other symbolic elements, such as the belief in fairies and the primary tooth, are counterbalanced decelerators, used by a mother to slow down the growing-up process. Mother and child subconsciously pull and push, respectively, as they jointly determine the degree of social maturity to be attributed to the tooth-losing child. The outcome is gradual, flexible, interactive, and dynamic. The flight toward maturity is not, by any means, straightforward, unidirectional, or mechanical, as a superficial application of Van Gennep's three stages might imply. There are symbolic and human forces of both drag and lift alike.

Considering the experience of children leads to the realization that the Tooth Fairy ritual holds much complexity of meaning. The custom helps the child to undergo unavoidable physical transformation involving some discomfort. At the same time, it helps the family to work through the child's new status as an older, more independent person. It is a remarkable paradox that the Fairy's delivery of money, the symbolic means that helps a child feel older, simultaneously helps the mother to perceive the child as still young, since still believing. Rituals to help children with family relationships or other problems are actively advocated by therapists.[14] Children naturally concoct rituals to make themselves feel comfortable at bedtime (stories, stuffed animals, special pillowcases, and so on), and parents willingly participate.[15] Often, imaginal experience is part and parcel of such rituals: sleeping with a special teddy bear friend, saying nighttime prayers, or expecting that the superheros depicted on the pillowcase will give protection. Understanding how such rituals work to ease the experience of all the individuals involved may well reveal dynamics as complex as those in the Tooth Fairy ritual.

As explained in the introduction to Van Gennep's *Rites of Passage,* the need for rituals still holds firm in contemporary times:

> There is no evidence that a secularized urban world has lessened the need for ritualized expression of an individual's transition from one status to another. . . . The critical problems of becoming male and female, or relations within the family, and of passing into old age are directly related to the devices which the society offers the individual to help him achieve the new adjustment.[16]

Far from trivial, the Tooth Fairy is a being who arrives on the scene during an important juncture in contemporary children's lives and delivers gifts (both tangible and spiritual) that are healing and enabling.

# Three

# Christmas and Easter:
## *Seasonal Rites of Passage with Modern Relevance*

May your days be merry and bright,
And may all your Christmases be white.
—Irving Berlin, "White Christmas"

When March the twenty-first is past
Just watch the silvery moon,
And when you see it full and round,
Know Easter'll be here soon.

After the moon has reached its full,
Then Easter will be here
On the very Sunday after
In each and every year.
—Anonymous, 1918

## RIGHT TIMING

Both Santa and the Easter Bunny are associated with seasonal holidays, or to put it more specifically, the seasonal rites of passage of Christmas and Easter. As anyone who has even indirectly participated in Christmas and Easter knows, these holidays provide us with a calendrical landmark that ushers in or marks the season.[1] Christmas and Easter help to give us our temporal bearings. Christmas coincides (at least approximately) with the winter solstice. Easter marks the advent of spring—in social meaning, if not always in climate.

Indeed, in tracing back the historical roots of modern Christmas and Easter celebrations, the ancient origins for these festivals are to be found in seasonal rites of passage. Historians mark the origins of contemporary Christmas at A.D. 601, when Pope Gregory set out to convert the Anglo-Saxons by ordering that the Anglo-Saxon winter feast be made a Christian festival. Anglo-Saxon local celebrations had originated in the Roman Saturnalia, a mid-December celebration ensuring solar renewal; the Saxon yule feast, celebrating the god Thor and the return of the sun at the winter solstice; and the seasonal holidays of the Druids.[2] Each of these ancient rites was timed to coincide with the winter solstice, when the sun reaches its lowest point in the sky and begins to rise again, a solar event sometimes referred to as the "birth of the sun."[3] As W. Lloyd Warner has elucidated, the winter solstice is the central point in a time that means night, coldness, rest, sleep, and sterility, as opposed to themes of day, light, warmth, activity, and liveliness associated with the period that commences with the vernal equinox.[4]

In *The Golden Bough*, Sir James Frazer alluded to the Christian church's intentions to "arbitrarily time" Easter (like Christmas) so as to "coincide with previously existing pagan festivals for the sake of weaning the heathen from their old faith."[5] Easter, Frazer maintained, superseded a vernal festival marking the death and resurrection of the vegetation god. A holiday now observed on the Sunday following the first full moon after the vernal equinox (some time between March 22 and April 25), Easter is thought to derive its very name from the Anglo-Saxon goddess of spring, Eostre. Eostre's festival was celebrated at the vernal equinox.[6] Both the hare and the egg were her symbols,[7] symbols of "the return to life after winter's sleep."[8] The name Easter may also derive from the Norse word for the spring season, Eostur.[9]

By ancient derivation as well as modern practice, then, Christmas and Easter are rites of passage that usher in or mark seasonal change. As will be emphasized later, Christmas and Easter contribute to a Van Gennepian rite of passage in another sense as well. Children who believe in (and later cease to believe in) Santa Claus and the Easter Bunny pass through a rite of passage on the way toward being grown up.[10]

## MODERN AMERICAN CHRISTMAS SYMBOLISM: HISTORICAL AND CULTURAL BACKGROUND

One can gain a helpful perspective on the significance of symbols associated with contemporary American Christmas and, specifically, the mythic figure of Santa Claus, by inquiring into their folkloric and historic origins. The constellation of customs that comprises modern American Christmas celebration (Christmas tree, gifts, Santa Claus, etc.) coalesced in America after the colonial period, indeed not until after the mid-nineteenth century.[11] During the seventeenth and eighteenth centuries, large groups of American colonists had opposed celebrating Christmas.[12] The Puritans outlawed Christmas (and Easter as well), imprisoning clergymen who preached on December 25 and fining parish officers who decorated the church.[13] Quakers, Baptists, Congregationalists, and Presbyterians joined in denouncing the observation of Christmas, on the grounds that the Bible did not ordain such celebration.[14] Some scholars have speculated that the Puritan opposition to Christmas may have contributed to the eventual secularization of Christmas, ironically enough, in that religious symbols (the Nativity, the Magi, the shepherds) became commingled with nonbiblical holiday symbols (such as Santa Claus).[15] In any case, the transition from "fast day" to "feast day," from "holy day" to "holiday," as Hutton Webster has aptly phrased it, was well under way by the mid-nineteenth century.[16]

Denominations once opposed to the celebration of Christmas gradually accepted the holiday in the course of the nineteenth century. During the middle decades of the 1800s, Santa Claus evolved to his modern American form and became the "dominant symbol" of the folk aspects of Christmas celebration.[17] Santa Claus—with his merriment reminiscent of the ancient Roman Saturnus and his magical travels resembling those of Thor—has nineteenth-century roots deriving from (1) the St. Nicholas festival of Dutch immigrants to America; (2) Clement Clark Moore's poem "A Visit from Saint Nicholas"; and (3) the illustrations of Thomas Nast.

St. Nicholas, patron saint of the chief winter festival of the Dutch, lived in Myra during the fourth century and was canonized in the ninth century. Associated with his life were a variety of legendary miraculous deeds, such as restoring the life of a drowned sailor and multiplying a supply of grain to provide adequate nutrition during famine.[18] After his death, Nicholas came to be known throughout Europe as a patron saint willing to intercede miraculously in dire events. Often these intercessions involved children, such as aiding a childless couple in the birth of a son or allowing a boy (kidnapped on the saint's feast day) to be miraculously returned to his parents one year later. When Dutch immigrants came to New York, they brought along St. Nicholas and his legends as well. St. Nicholas was said to have "presided at the figure-head of the first emigrant ship that touched [New York] shores."[19] The Dutch also brought to America the custom of filling children's shoes, festively left out on the eve of December 6, St. Nicholas's feast day, with gifts. This custom the post-Reformationist Calvinist Walich Siewerts criticized in strong terms, much as the American Puritans had condemned Christmas:

> It is a foolish and pointless custom to fill children's shoes with all sorts of sweets and nonsense. What else is this but sacrifice to an idol? Those who do it do not seem to understand what true religion is.[20]

Despite Siewerts's Calvinist condemnation, December 6 was retained when the Dutch arrived in America, as the day in honor of Sinter Klaas (a form of the Dutch "Sint Nikolass"). On American shores, the name Sinter Klaas gradually became anglicized into Santa Claus under the increasing influence of English colonists.[21] In the melting pot of America, the feast day of St. Nicholas was sometimes shifted via cross-cultural contact to Christmas Eve or New Year's Eve, such that

> By 1820 the United States possessed this tale of a popular "saint" who visited children on December 5th, 24th, or 31st, as a magical gift bringer. He traveled on horseback, in a wagon, or even walked. In some accounts he came down the chimney and placed presents in the shoes or stockings of good children and switches in those of bad.[22]

The Christmas scholar James Barnett credits Clement Clark Moore's 1822 poem "A Visit from Saint Nicholas" with crystalizing popular notions of Santa Claus and with blending the traditional St. Nicholas with other folk motifs, including elves and brownies, sleigh and reindeer. Moore was an ordained minister and a professor at the General Theological Seminary in New York when he penned the poem to read to his six children on Christmas Eve. A copy was eventually sent without Dr. Moore's permission to the *Troy Sentinel* (New York). It was printed anonymously, under this foreword:

> We know not to whom we are indebted for the following description of that unwearied patron of children—that homely but delightful personification of parental kindness—Santa Claus, his costume and his equipage, as he hops about visiting the firesides of this happy land, laden with Christmas bounties; but from whomsoever it may have come, we give thanks for it.[23]

Although the poem was republished twelve times in the first ten years (including in two almanacs for the year 1824), Moore did not acknowledge authorship of the poem until 1848.[24]

After Moore's poem was published, a number of American artists began to visually portray the emerging figure of Santa Claus, in versions that varied greatly.[25] A drawing by Fredericks in 1870, for instance, depicted Santa Claus as resembling a Druid priest who wore white, flowing robes, a stern expression, and a wreath of holly. But it was cartoonist Thomas Nast who was "primarily responsible for the fat and rosy-cheeked appearance of our modern Santa."[26] From 1863 to 1886, Nast did a series of cartoon drawings for *Harper's Weekly* in which Santa Claus evolved from the fat little elflike creature of Dr. Moore's poem into the full-bodied, bearded, fur-attired, jolly persona that has become a fixture of modern times. In the picture *Santa Claus His Works,* Nast showed how Santa spends his entire year, making toys, spying on children, pausing atop a chimney, driving his magical sleigh through the sky, and so on. Nast's conception of Santa became the accepted stereotype of the gift bringer by the latter part of the nineteenth century.[27]

In his book *Centuries of Childhood,* Philippe Ariès attributes the emergence and popular acceptance of St. Nicholas and Santa Claus to the increased cultural role of family celebrations and the reduced importance of great collective festivals that occurred along with Western industrialization.[28] The societal need under conditions of modern industrialization for festivals that celebrate the family is also identified by Brian Sutton-Smith.

Three hundred years ago the family was the center of most work life, most political life, most religious life, any educational life, and most reproductive life. [After industrialization] in this century, most of these functions are attended to elsewhere. There are factories, political parties, churches, schools. . . . It is not surprising, therefore, to find both that the family is in crisis, and that the major holidays in modern society help to enhance the value of the family to its members. On Thanksgiving and Christmas, in particular, we can attempt to recover from the divisive effects of the modern world, and put our family world together once again—Holidays bring together those whose relationships the pressures of life cause to fall apart.[29]

If American conceptions of Santa Claus crystallized during America's industrializing period of the nineteenth century, helped along by the creativity of Moore and Nast, it is not surprising that Christmas continues to be celebrated in the twentieth century when the "long-term decline in the significance of the family as a social institution" has continued or even accelerated.[30] Of course, this does not mean that the symbolism inherent in the Santa Claus myth has remained entirely unchanged. Present-day children (as Barnett anticipated in 1954) perceive the reindeer Rudolph, not mentioned in Moore's poem, to be an important element that has "fused with Santa Claus in Christmas lore."[31] Rudolph illustrates that twentieth-century impressions of Santa Claus have evolved, selectively incorporating elements from popular culture.

The story of Rudolph the Red-Nosed Reindeer was written in 1939 by an employee of Montgomery Ward, then a mail-order firm.[32] The employee, named Robert L. May, was assigned to write a Christmas "animal story," and he decided to organize the narrative around the ugly duckling motif. The story of the outcast red-nosed reindeer, who becomes Santa's valued lead sleigh-puller because his nose can illuminate the sky, became a promo-tional leaflet, of which 2,400,000 copies were distributed in 1939. The story was introduced on a commercial basis in 1947. In 1949 a song about Rudolph was composed by Johnny Marks and quickly became popular. Rudolph came to receive numerous letters from children and indirectly to impact perceptions of Santa himself. As Barnett writes:

> In May's story Santa Claus was different from St. Nicholas of Moore's poem in that he was not omnipotent, could not see perfectly in the darkness, and sought the help of a young reindeer (read "child"). Symbolically, the small child came to the aid of the powerful parents and exhibited unexpected pow-ers. . . . The possibility that children identify with Rudolph offers an explanation of the sudden and continuing popularity of the story, the song, and the various pictorial representations of the now-famous deer.[33]

## CONTEMPORARY CULTURAL STATUS OF CHRISTMAS

Modern-day sociologists have studied Christmas and its gift giv-ing, taking a somewhat functionalist view that Christmas serves to celebrate and affirm family bonds and sociability. For example, Theodore Caplow and his collaborators conducted a replication of Robert and Helen Lynd's famed "Middletown" study in Muncie, Indiana, during the 1970s.[34] In the revisited Middletown studies, one focus of interest was the contemporary festival cycle, the series of American holidays and special occasions associated with particular symbols and prescribed behaviors. Christmas, judged to be "unquestionably Middletown's most important holiday," was said to encompass two major themes.[35] First, there is the maintenance of social bonds via gift giving. Second, there is the theme of nurturing children, personified by Santa Claus as the grandparental figure who "receives nothing for his generosity."[36]

As revealed by Caplow's data, parents expect to give more valuable and more numerous gifts to their minor children (and to their adult children living at home) than they receive. As Caplow and his fellow researchers state, "this imbalance is central to the entire ritual," since "the theme of unreciprocated giving provides one of the few connections between the secular and religious iconography of the festival—the Three Wise Men coming from a distant land to bring unreciprocated gifts to a child."[37] Of course, through the guise of the Santa Claus ritual, unreciprocated giving to children is magnified to the extreme. Santa epitomizes nurturing and generosity. He lives in the cold, bitter, arctic world of the North Pole, and yet Santa and his home convey warmth, jolliness, and cheer. Santa, with his cheerful wife and merry elves, sets family warmth in stark contrast to the cold outside weather.

Given the sociological conclusion that contemporary American Christmas customs affirm social relationships, particularly family relationships, and celebrate loving nurturance of children, note that similar conclusions have also been drawn by other contemporary investigators. Elizabeth Hirschman and Priscilla LaBarbara, who conducted research among business students and among Evangelical Christians, concluded that "Christmas is a celebration and commemoration of family life."[38] The ideology inherent in Christmas celebration—love for kin in general and children in particular—reflects themes consistent with femininity in American culture,[39] and with the private realm of the family. Intriguingly, this system of meaning may have evolved more and more in a family direction in recent history; a content analysis of Middletown newspapers revealed that "Christmas had become less a civic festival and more a family festival between the 1920s and the 1970s."[40]

Not all scholars studying Christmas have come to the unqualified conclusion of Caplow and his associates that Christmas and Christmas gift giving celebrate family bonds and sociability. To be sure, a positive theme recurs across studies: the sense of communality and sentiment for others' welfare. But negative themes have been associated with Christmas as well. Russell Belk has argued that there is a materialistic, greedy, selfish underside to gift giving during the Christmas festival and that Santa Claus is the "God of materialism and hedonism."[41]

Hirschman and LaBarbara posit a bipolarity in the meaning of Christmas gift giving. At one pole of meaning lie "sacred interpersonal bonds," such sentiments as "showing people through presents that you care about them," or giving "presents to each other to represent the gladness and celebration of Christ's birth." At the opposite pole of meaning lie "selfish, secular interests" expressed in such comments as "I enjoy receiving gifts, but would be willing to forego that to be released of the burden and expense of buying gifts for others." Hirschman and LaBarbara propose that

> Many consumers cannot create bonds of fellowship and communion, experience feelings of generosity and nurturance, and open up their hearts, souls and senses when these aspects of themselves have lain dormant for so long. Sadly, one of the . . . costs of modern man's independence and individuality may be the existential angst and loneliness in which he has become suspended.[42]

Psychoanalytically oriented writers agree that for some people the idealized family togetherness associated with Christmas is hard to achieve.[43] For people who have difficulty with intimate family relationships (e.g., a history of divorce or parental death), a "holiday syndrome" can develop that predisposes a person to "deny the meaningfulness of the holiday season to him, though the emotional components and unconsciously motivated behavior remains."[44] Renzo Sereno goes so far as to severely criticize the Santa Claus custom as "an adult affair which children are dragged into, under stress and under rigid rules" in order that the adult might "delude himself on his own actual feelings of loneliness."[45] Case histories of patients with "Christmas neuroses" are cited by psychoanalytic writers to support the view that Christmas can be a negative experience.[46]

Insofar as Christmas (and Santa Claus) constitutes a family ritual, Christmas holiday practices and emotions are necessarily embedded within the particular family milieu in which they arise.

In some cases, that milieu may indeed be conducive to depression and neurosis, especially in cases receiving clinical attention.

James Bossard and Eleanor Boll have remarked that family ritual, in general, is "a relatively reliable index of family integration."[47] Families that are well-knit, that function smoothly as a unit, that are harmonious rather than tension ridden, tend to have well-established rituals and traditions. These rituals help to maintain common family values, which in turn contribute to family unity. Christmas ritual practices—directly *symbolizing* love of family and nurturing of children—are doubly reflective cases for Bossard and Boll's link between ritual and family integration.

Christmas rituals help a family to tie the past to the present, by repeating a behavior so that the present recalls the past. This brings a sort of temporal unity to family experience via repeated reenactment.[48] The rich meaning that can arise from reenacted behavior is illustrated by two anecdotes, taken from works on family ritual.

> When Kay S. was three years old, her father held her on his lap and read to her on Christmas Eve Clement Moore's well-known poem, "A Visit from St. Nicholas." Each Christmas Eve since, this has been repeated. When Kay was five years old her sister Jane was born, and during the succeeding years the reading of this poem on Christmas Eve became more and more of a ceremonial event. As the two daughters became older, they would sit on either side of the father on the family sofa, and mother and other relatives would be present. After the reading, refreshments came to be served, and talk would follow about Christmas celebrations of former years. As time went on, the ceremony became more and more elaborate. Candles were lit while other lights were extinguished; and the conversational aftermath lengthened. Nothing ever deterred Kay and Jane from being at home on Christmas Eve; dates with boys, even after their engagements had been announced, were not made; once Kay did not accept an invitation to a much desired trip so that she might be at home for "the reading." After Kay's marriage, she and her husband came to her parents' home on Christmas Eve in order to be present for the event. This prac-

tice has been continued down to the present time, both by
Kay and her husband and by Jane and her husband. Last year,
the father read to both daughters, their husbands, three grand-
children and grandmother.[49]

## The Christmas Cake
### (Hattie Davis, Age 68)

I tell you one thing. . . . every year we were children, my
mother used to bake a large cake, and after she got so she
couldn't bake it, she'd have it baked up there at a bakery. But
she baked this cake and one Christmas we all stood around
this cake and sang "Happy Birthday, dear Jesus. We are so
glad you were born today. Happy Birthday, dear Jesus." My
mother is still alive and we still do that every year.[50]

If, as Lloyd Warner writes, the family is the seat of contemporary
American symbolic life,[51] Christmas emerges as the central American festival that celebrates the family. The felt importance of
family-derived rituals at Christmas has been attributed by Caplow
and others to the fact that the family is the institution most at
risk in contemporary American society, since it is the institution
most dependent on emotions (rather than reason) for its continu-
ance.[52] Brian Sutton-Smith echoes this view in *Toys as Culture*.

> Holidays are most likely to reflect those parts of society where
> the pressures and conflicts are felt to be the greatest. Thus, in
> the past, when class divisions were a great burden, the festival
> was likely to be a reversal of that class division, as in the
> traditional Mardi Gras, where the "lowly" people pretend to
> be kings and often did insult and even injury to those who
> were of higher status. . . . But if class division was what was
> held together in the old festivals and celebrated by its reversal
> on those occasions, and if festivals usually reveal the major
> conflicts in any given society, then we might conclude from
> the modern tendency of turning all festivals into family festi-
> vals, that the family is the endangered species of modern social
> forms. Perhaps we have these family festivals because we fear
> that, in the modern world, the family is falling apart.[53]

Perhaps partly because of its family-supportive meaning, Christmas is a festival whose relevance to modern life has led to "growing popularity of the event not only here where it was developed, but also among populations elsewhere, such as Japan."[54] The cross-cultural transmission of Christmas may also be partly due to the consonance of Christmas symbols with contemporary consumer culture and its hedonistic spending. As Belk puts it, Christmas "preserves the Cratchit-like values of spending, lavishness and hedonism . . . without invoking the Scrooge-like values of selfishness, love of money, and avarice."[55] Christmas mediates between hedonism and selfless love, especially love of children, upon whom material goods are lavished. On the face of it, hedonism (for example, lavish parties with fancy clothing), and selfless giving (in the form of charity toward children and others), are paradoxical values; yet Christmas manages to encompass both indulgence and sacrifice at once.

## MODERN AMERICAN EASTER SYMBOLISM: HISTORICAL AND CULTURAL BACKGROUND

Historical accounts of the evolution of contemporary American Easter practices are less detailed and definitive than for Santa Claus and Christmas. Barnett notes that Easter was celebrated in America as early as 1855.[56] He quotes the following statement, which appeared in the *New York Daily Tribune* in 1868:

> The Easter festival, once allowed to pass almost unnoticed by our Knickerbocker and Puritan ancestors, is yearly more and more observed and was celebrated with greater interest than has hitherto been manifested.[57]

Robert Myers reports that early Puritan colonists tried to "play down the observance of Easter as far as possible," just as they had for Christmas.[58] During the Civil War period, a movement began (led by the Presbyterians) to reinstate the observance of Easter in America, so as to provide "renewed hope for those bereaved by war."[59] With the revival of Easter as a festival, customs that had emigrated from Europe, such as the German tradition of building nests for the Easter rabbit, hiding the nests in the barn or around the house, and encouraging children to believe that (if they were good) the "rabbit would lay Easter eggs in the nests," began to be disseminated.[60]

It is widely reported that both Easter eggs and the Easter rabbit or Easter hare derive from symbolic referents in the distant, pre-Christian past.[61] T. Sharper Knowlson points out that "all the nations of antiquity—the Egyptians, Persians, Romans, Greeks, Gauls and others—regarded the egg as an emblem of the universe—a work of supreme Divinity."[62] Hindu mythology tells of the World-Egg that was formed in the beginning of the universe and that "split asunder" to form two eggshell parts, one gold, one silver.[63] The widespread and ancient symbolic association between new life and the apparently dead egg from which that life sprang suggests that an egg is a universally available symbol of renewal and rebirth. Eggs were said to be dyed and eaten at the spring festivals in ancient Egypt, Persia, Greece, and Rome; ancient Persians gave eggs as gifts during the vernal equinox.[64] There is speculation that missionaries or knights of the Crusades brought the tradition of coloring eggs westward. At any rate, customs involving Easter eggs are recorded in western Europe beginning in the fifteenth century.[65]

As for the bearer of Easter eggs, the Easter Bunny, note that it has not universally been the hare or the rabbit that serves as the deliverer of Easter eggs. Newall writes:

> The hare . . . is often displaced by other egg-bringers. Westphalians have an Easter fox and birds are a widespread substitute—or really, a more obvious choice. Swiss children believe it is the cuckoo, and in Styria, though the hare tradition has recently been adopted, they also prepare nests for the red-egg bird. . . . Other popular birds are the Tyrolese Easter chicken and the rooster of Schleswig-Holstein, which lays red eggs on Easter morning.[66]

Still, anomalous as an egg-bearing rabbit may be, the bearer of Easter eggs in contemporary America derives from the German hare or rabbit. To be perfectly correct, it is the hare, not the rabbit, that relates historically to Easter. The hare is a nocturnal creature thought never to blink or to close its eyes and is therefore associated with the moon, the very celestial body whose phase changing sets the date for the timing of Easter. A widely attested belief among peoples of inner Asia, south Asia, east Asia, North America, Mesoamerica, and southern Africa asserts that a rabbit or hare dwells in the moon.[67] At the time of early Christians, rabbits were common images used in funerary art, for example, on gravestones, as symbols of mortality.[68] If modern Easter eggs represent the source of life, the Easter Bunny also represents archaic religious values that are continuous with ancient beliefs.[69]

## CONTEMPORARY CULTURAL STATUS OF EASTER

Although both Christmas and Easter have a dual religious-secular symbolic structure, research of recent practices shows that Easter celebrations are less secular and less commercialized than Christmas celebrations.[70] Included in the celebration of Easter are the giving of gifts, such as Easter baskets filled with colored eggs and candy, flowers, and young animals (ducklings, chicks, and bunnies); the Easter egg hunt, in which parents hide eggs for their children to find; Easter dinner, which unlike Christmas dinner, has no precisely prescribed menu; and the Easter Bunny.

Gift giving at Easter does not clearly specify or mark social ties, as it does at Christmas. Gifts "may be given from anyone to anyone."[71] Roles are undifferentiated and impersonal in the Easter egg hunt; the eggs are given in a highly indirect manner so that no one establishes or affirms a tie with anyone else.

Ambiguity, in fact, abounds in Easter customs. The eggs themselves are ambiguous, allegedly produced by a (male) rabbit, rather than a (female) bird.[72] And rabbits represent ambiguous, enigmatic animals. As Theodore Caplow and Margaret Williamson assert, a rabbit fits *all* the categories of animals recognized in "Middletown"; the category of domestic-inedible (pet), the category of wild-edible, the category of domestic-edible, and the category of wild-inedible.[73] Animals that are intermediate, ambiguous entities are apt to be credited with potency, sacredness, and worthiness of fear and worship, as Edmund Leach has demonstrated.[74] Rabbits are difficult to sex (albeit fertile) and have baby forms less distinguishable from adult forms than are chicks, ducklings, and lambs from their adult forms.[75] Overall, the Easter Bunny is ideally suited to "represent the confusion and blurring of social roles in the presence of nature," a theme consistent with the meaning system of Easter.[76] Easter celebrates an ambiguity: the idea that death can be life, that resurrection can deny death's existence. With the exception of pastel colors, new clothing, and eggs (which fairly clearly denote new life), Easter symbolism contains ambiguous meanings, suggesting a focus on the merged whole, rather than the specified parts. As the "Middletown" investigators argue:

> Its symbols and activities convey the idea that the cultural distinctions that Middletown recognizes—pet or farm animal, male or female, parent or child, life or death—need not ultimately be distinguished since all belong to the whole of Middletown's view of the world. . . . Christmas takes the world apart and identifies each part; Easter reassembles it and refrains from identifying anything.[77]

Another contrast between Christmas and Easter raised by Caplow's research team involves the role of children in the secular ritual. At Christmas, the dependence of children is emphasized in conjunction with the aforementioned theme of child nurturance. Children are essentially passive in the Santa Claus ritual, tucked into bed with special care on Christmas Eve after hanging up empty stockings. The religious iconography also represents children as passively dependent creatures: A dependent baby Jesus was wrapped in swaddling clothes and laid in a manger. By comparison, children at Easter are urged to be independent, to go out and do for themselves in the competitive action of the Easter egg hunt and, I might add, in the act of coloring their own eggs. Caplow argues that Easter and Christmas attempt, in opposing ways, to resolve a fundamental contradiction universal to human life: that children will ultimately need to be independent, after a long phase of almost total dependence.[78]

# Four

# The Christmas Spirit:
# *Santa Claus and Christmas*

As children, in the brief years of belief, we
take Santa for granted, in the same way we rely
on our parents' love. It is only afterward that he is
truly cherished. When you're a child he brings you
presents. When you're older he brings much more.
Like other legendary, mythological creatures, or the
saints of old, he is simply who we need him to be,
evolving with us and filling our need for magic, amazement
and surprise. The magic dust comes down the chimney,
and jolly as ever and covered with soot, he takes shape
before our very eyes.
—Mary Haley

On Christmas morning my little sister Sarah and I opened our presents.
When it looked as if everything had been unwrapped, Sarah found one
last small box behind the tree. . . . Inside was the silver bell! . . . I
shook the bell. It made the most beautiful sound my sister and I had
ever heard.
But my mother said, "Oh that's too bad." "Yes," said my father,
"it's broken."
When I'd shaken the bell, my parents had not heard a
sound.
At one time most of my friends could hear the bell,
but as years passed, it fell silent for all of them. Even
Sarah found one Christmas that she could no longer
hear its sweet sound. Though I've grown old, the
bell still rings for me as it does for all who truly
believe.
—Chris Van Allsburg, *The Polar Express*

## CHILDLIKE FAITH (SEASONALLY) REVISITED

Within American culture, Christmas represents a holiday of child-oriented enchantment, of juvenile uplifting surprise. In J. M. Barrie's play *Peter Pan,* for example, Christmas is presented as literally uplifting. Pan instructs the Darling children in how to fly; to do so, they must "think lovely wonderful thoughts." So instructed, Christmas is one of the first ideas the Darling children think of, sufficiently lovely indeed to invoke flight.

As one six-year-old told me, Christmas is a "surprise for kids." Generally, children know that much hoopla and preparation has been geared to their interests at Christmastime. Santa Claus and Christmas in general are tilted in a child's direction. To fully understand children's perspectives on Christmas, though, consider that in another sense Christmas is a predictable fact of life. To youngsters, the enchantment of receiving many gifts and much attention at Christmas is not necessarily out of the ordinary. This was a striking realization to Mrs. Lind, who kept field notes on her children.

> What is remarkable to me this year is in what the kids did not say. For example [my six-year-old daughter] got a dollhouse from us and dolls for the house from Santa. No questions about how Santa knew she was getting the house. No surprise one way or the other at the quantity of things from Santa—less than in previous years (they each had a big present from us) but apparently adequate. A very matter-of-fact attitude, like they had expected he'd come and he did and that was that.

In other words, children are less mystified and amazed about Christmas customs than adult perception would predict. In the world of a typical preschooler or kindergartner, magic and awesome abilities are a wide-ranging fact of life. In a typical interview exchange, Tina, age six, talked in quick succession of magical snowmen, visionary reindeer, and a magical Mickey Mouse (who, in her mind, may well be a friend of the magical Santa Claus), among others—giving the impression that the world is crowded with enchantment. But she was simply reporting this to me, rather than expressing awe or wonder about it.

CDC: What's that snowman doing [in a Christmas decoration]?

TINA: He's got his hat up like this and bowing.

CDC: Anything special about that snowman?

TINA: Maybe it's Frosty and he has a magic hat.

CDC: Frosty the Snowman has a magic hat?

TINA: Yeah. And if you take the hat off, he'll froze. I mean, yeah, he'll froze. But if you put the hat back on, he'll come alive again. . . . I don't believe snowmen can talk. Maybe at the North Pole, but I don't know. . . . Santa Claus might make a snowman and he might put magic on him, and he'll come alive. . . .

CDC: Is that Rudolph right there [pointing to decoration]?

TINA: No, that's just a plain old deer.

CDC: What's the difference?

TINA: He doesn't have a red nose, like a big red nose. . . . If there's really a big fog, he can light up his nose and then he'll show Santa the way.

CDC: Why wouldn't Santa be able to find his own way through the fog?

TINA: Because there's no other reindeer that has a red nose. The reindeers, they might, like, fall down in the fog. . . .

CDC: You've also got this one [decoration] up here of Snow White and the Seven Dwarfs. . . . You've got a lot of [decorations] that are from Disney. Do they seem like things that would belong on a Christmas tree? . . .

TINA: Because maybe Mickey's magic, and maybe Santa Claus is magic. Maybe they get along together. Like maybe they're friends.

At another point, Tina said that she has seen signs of reindeer hooves in her mother's room: "I found . . . a little circle in my mommy's room, that the reindeer paw, like bounced there." Yet again, this did not seem awe inspiring to her so much as it seemed evidence, pure and simple.

For the most part, children take their faith in stride. If anything, it is adults who are wide-eyed (vicariously) at the fantastic, mystical events of Christmas and Santa. Children rarely if ever commented during interviews on how "amazing" or "wonderful" the happenings of Christmas are. Rather, it is adults who repeatedly labeled children as "excited" or full of "wonder." One mother commented,

> I guess I enjoy seeing them be excited. And the joy in their eyes. The wonderment. The excitement in their eyes. . . . It's the idea that somebody drives around the whole world on a sled. Come on. Give me a break. The fact that idea, he could really do that in a day. When you think about it, it's kind of overwhelming.

Another mother observed,

> Just as an adult, [Christmas] doesn't mean that much, as an adult. But when you have kids into it . . . [Whispers so as not to be overheard.] Just like yesterday [Christmas] when they got up and were just so excited and . . . were dancing around and they couldn't wait for us. Because I told them they had to make their beds. And you could just hear their feet barely touching the ground [laughter]. They were just so excited. They wanted to get down here [to the living room]. And you know, it adds so much more to it than if we would just wake up by ourselves and come down.

As adults conspire to bring about eye-widening excitement and wonder in their children each Christmas, what matters seems to be that adults perceive such reactions in young ones—whether or not children themselves treat the whole affair as more flat and factual than awe inspiring. Ironically, a child-centered investigation of American customs reveals that Christmas is less a holiday for children than native explication insists. Rather, *Christmas is a holiday in which other members of the culture socially situate themselves vis-à-vis children.* This includes reinforcing the social responsibilities and privileges of grandparents, parents, older siblings, and others (who participate in the expense and effort of "doing Christmas" for children). Further, since children symbolize, within the web of cultural meanings in America, such qualities as wonder, faith, and the continuing importance and need for the nuclear family, "childlike" qualities such as wonder, awe, and suspension of disbelief toward unseen forces become magnified and modeled at Christmas.

In adults' perceptions, children's excitement at Christmas is made possible by the unique juvenile capacity to see beyond the world as it is and to suspend disbelief so as to allow for magic and fantasy. As the title of a recent popular television show suggests, early childhood years are "the wonder years" in the modern American age-grade schematic. The capacity for fantasy and wonder is expected to be short-lived, restricted to the early years of life, when mystical events are still thought possible. *The Nutcracker* ballet, Santa Claus, and the Disney characters, which feature prominently in the yuletide iconography, all reinforce the sense of wonder and surprise, the stretching toward the magical and unknown for a brief stage early in the life cycle. When families encourage this stage for their children through the rituals of Christmas, they symbolically validate for themselves the importance of wonder and transcendent reality in general. Such interests are evident in the remarks of these two mothers:

> I think [visiting Santa Claus] is good for them. I don't think it's bad for kids to have the feeling that there's a little magic around. . . . Let them believe that something magic is around and out there. Plus, I still believe there is myself [laughter]. You know, I think there's more to this life than just exactly what you see. . . . I mean God, I mean another plane. I mean, yeah, I believe there's forces working beyond us. I believe . . . there is reincarnation, and I've lived other lives, till I reach a perfection, whatever you call that.

> It was always so magical to me as a child. So I guess it's what I tried to get my kids to see, the magic. . . . I don't know if we can even recapture it. . . . I would like them to have that naïveté and be able to be totally surprised. . . . [Eyes well up in tears. CDC: Now I'm beginning to think that in some way you believe in Santa Claus.] Yeah! . . . My husband and I . . . both of us have always done the big surprise Christmas morning . . . even before we had kids. . . . It was that total magic, all of a sudden there's tons of stuff under the tree.

The tendency of Americans to associate childhood with fantastic thinking and belief in magical phenomena traces back to the early part of this century, if not farther. In 1932 Margaret Mead contrasted the United States—where, as she put it, "traditional animistic material which is decried by modern scientific thinking is still regarded as appropriate material for child training"—with the Manus culture, in which "the adult culture . . . provides each generation grown to maturity with a set of traditional animistic concepts [but] provides the children with no background for animistic constructs."[1] In other words, in both groups certain types of thought processes were acceptable for one age group but not another. But the pattern for what thought processes were acceptable is culture specific: Age-graded belief structures are culturally relative. What goes among American children (wonder and magic) does not go among Manus children.

In contemporary America, belief in Santa Claus is generally expected by adults to be limited to the period of early childhood. An expected rite of passage out of childhood, disillusionment in Santa is a step that can bring sadness and grieving to parents.[2] When kids stop believing in Santa Claus, parents recognize that their child has reached a more "mature" life stage. Anthropologist Claude Lévi-Strauss recognized this in the European Santa figure, Father Christmas.

> Father Christmas first of all expresses the difference in status between small children on the one hand and adolescents and adults on the other. In this respect he is part of a vast array of beliefs and practices that anthropologists have studied to understand the rites of passage and initiation. In fact there are very few societies where in one way or another children (and sometimes women as well) are not excluded from the company of men by their ignorance of certain secrets of their belief— carefully fostered—in some illusion which adults reveal at the opportune moment, thereby sanctioning the admission of the younger generation to their own.[3]

Disbelief in Santa Claus (a conclusion American children generally reach on their own, rather than out of revelation by an adult)

constitutes an anticipated, inevitable event of youthful development. Older siblings who have made the leap of nonfaith often
take on the grown-up role to help perpetuate the Santa custom
for younger children. One nonbelieving older brother in this
study, for example, began climbing up on the roof and making
"reindeer noises" each Christmas Eve. Or older kids might play
Santa by dressing the part at parties, or by replying to letters to
Santa, or by helping to fill stockings.

As a residual of having given up belief in Santa Claus, a nostalgia for this "simpler time," when the world was unadulterated (in
the fullest possible sense) and filled with magic, often remains
into adulthood. It is this nostalgia for the golden age of childhood,
no doubt, which is cathartically released upon having one's own
children and playing Santa Claus for them. American adults idealize both the developmental past (that is, early childhood) and
the historical past, an era of fireplaces and sleigh rides. As the
developmental and historical pasts are rendered innocent, Christmas, with its Currier and Ives nostalgia and its child-centered
customs, resonates with and reinforces the idealization. This is a
case of returning to a paradisal world, a golden age such as Mircea
Eliade described.

> Man desires to recover the active presence of the gods; he also
> desires to live in the world as it came from the Creator's hands,
> fresh, pure and strong. It is the nostalgia for the perfection of
> beginnings that chiefly explains the periodic return. . . . We
> may say that the desire to live in the divine presence and in a
> perfect world (perfect because newly born) corresponds to the
> nostalgia for a paradisal situation.[4]

Discussion of the Santa Claus custom by adult informants reveals
that a paradisaic sentiment indeed pervades this periodically returning, godlike benefactor.

> I wonder why my kids are into fantasy. I love fantasy myself
> and that whole child feeling, that whole childhood concept of
> getting whatever you, everything you possibly could want from
> this wonderful person who does all these wonderful things for
> you.

Maybe 'cause we're all kids at heart, me and my husband . . .
I don't think we're ever gonna grow up. I mean, to us, we
always get all enthused. . . . Sometimes I wish there was . . .
somebody to give you everything you wanted all the time.

Everybody says, like as adults, when you believed in Santa
Claus, then you were innocent and young. And people want
to go back. They use that to capture something that they've
lost by being older. They say, when I used to believe in Santa
Claus, if I could go back to that time. It's just a way of recaptur-
ing your youth and your . . . innocence, when you had no
stresses and life was wonderful.

In a society whose predominant adult ethos is scientific empiri-
cism and technological materialism, Santa Claus tales (like the
Easter Bunny, the Tooth Fairy, or even fairy tales) in effect form
an age-restricted cultural reservoir for supernatural folk beliefs.[5]
From an adult perspective, the childhood myth is by virtue of its
age restrictiveness a "mock" mythology; the "gods" contained in
the juvenile pantheon are culturally labeled as suitable for the
naive, unsocialized young. Adults can remain skeptical and yet
have the vicarious benefit of seeing their children believe.[6]

If relinquishing belief in Santa Claus provides a personal, ego-
centric (that is, individually centered) rite of passage along the
course of growing up, then, the Santa Claus custom simultaneously provides a sociocentric (i.e., socially centered) ritual. In
sociocentric terms, the custom orients nonchildren toward children, recalling the symbolic association of children with wonder,
awe, and an idyllic golden age. Such experiences are largely ex-
cluded from the adult workaday world. The childhood cult of
Santa Claus is a reservoir for the human capacity to suspend
rational disbelief and to experience wonder at the unknowable,
the transcendent. As such, Santa is not solely a childhood cult at
all, but a ritual by which both adults and children are touched
through expressive symbolism.

## SANTA CLAUS

To study Christmas among children is to take an imaginal journey
up (to the roof top, or the North Pole). Along the way, reindeer,

flying sleigh, elves, presents, and a godlike figure in a red suit, whose whole purpose is generosity toward children, present themselves. Among the "presented" icons, Santa's gifts of toys are particularly prominent features when children describe events. Often, when informant children were asked to "tell me about Christmas," they began by describing or showing me the toys they had received. Generally, toys and other presents were central to their discussion of the holiday.

CDC: Tell me everything that happens at Christmas.

JANE (age six): You get lots of presents and Santa comes.

CDC: Why do we have Christmas?

JOHN (age six): To get new toys and stuff.

Children imagine that if they visited the North Pole (in their cosmology, a place above the rest of the earth but below heaven), they would spend their time making toys with Santa and the elves. "What would you do if you visited Santa at the North Pole?" was a question I posed.

[Girl, seven:] I would think I'd go make a doll for myself with him. A real pretty doll [gleeful laughter]. I think that's what I would do.

[Girl, six:] Make toys for him and help him.

[Boy, seven:] We'd play with him, try to help the elves make the toys.

[Boy, seven:] I would help the elves, I would help [them] work.

The costumed Santa at the shopping mall undoubtedly reinforces the salience of toys and other gifts as an element of Christmas. The Santa impersonator observed in this study never failed to give a visiting child a free gift (a cardboard Christmas tree with stickers for ornaments). And only a few very young infants were not asked by Santa to tell their "list" of desired gifts. Without fail, children old enough to be linguistically competent were asked, "What do you want for Christmas?" If children had no answer of their own to this question, Santa prompted them with gender-constraining suggestions: "How about some trucks and cars?"—to boys—or "How about a new dolly?"—to girls. Santa even asked a child what her stuffed animal, carried along with her, wanted for Christmas.

Clearly, the role of Santa, to give gifts wanted by the child, is a core representation within the Christmas idiom. Ever since Marcel Mauss pondered gift giving as a process that integrates society,[7] gift giving has been explained by anthropologists as an expressive act betokening social relationships. Barry Schwartz has stated that gifts have a socializing function of imposing a giver-derived identity upon the recipient, as exemplified by the gender role expectations that certain gifts (e.g., toy vehicles for boys, dolls for girls) symbolically carry. Unreciprocated gifts from Santa Claus, in Schwartz's view, impose forceful social control.

> Parents are especially aware of the fact that the child pays the cost of social inferiority when he accepts a gift from them and fails to reciprocate. . . . This principle is perhaps nowhere better seen than through the character of Santa Claus, the greatest of all gift givers, whose powers of surveillance and ability to grant and withhold benefits are annually exploited by parents as instruments of control over children.[8]

Yet the consistency with which the Santa impersonator asks the child what they want demonstrates that the child is actually far from passive in the process of Santa's gift giving. As explained earlier, parents derive vicarious pleasure from seeing their child in a state of extreme joy, encoding, for parents, wonder and awe over Santa's gift delivery. To enable such a vicarious thrill, the child must eagerly welcome—not reluctantly accept, or worse, reject—the selected gifts. Parents carefully weigh children's reactions to a gift in selecting it. Children indirectly dictate Santa's gift selection by means of their anticipated reactions to the gift. For instance, survey research has shown that children who prefer gender-typed toys are more likely to receive such gifts than children who prefer cross-gender toys.[9]

Far from powerless in the transaction, children send millions of letters (not all of which are part of the official postal system's mail) to the North Pole, testifying to children's perceived sense of influence in the gift process. Indeed, some schools incorporate "writing to Santa" to request certain gifts as a ritualized class assignment. As Mrs. Elwell, the mother of one second-grader, described it:

> At school they had them all write letters to Santa [in second grade]. . . . Then [my son] got a little reply back. One of the older kids wrote a letter for the answer. And he was satisfied that Santa knew what he wanted.

Mothers may not follow children's lists to the letter when selecting gifts for Santa to bring, but they treat such lists seriously, sometimes even participating in their preparation, as Mrs. Marshall did:

> We sit down and we go through the wish book, the Sears wish book or the Penney's wish book. We sit down like in November and we make a list. . . . He doesn't bring it with him when he goes to see Santa. I try and have him remember what he wants.

Nor are children fully passive, in point of fact, in the gift transaction between themselves and Santa. Leaving cookies and milk for Santa to eat and drink is a widespread practice.[10] Santa's gifts are reciprocated by means of this offering, and the element of reciprocity ("It's a kind of giving") is welcomed by mothers. Often the reindeer are included in the offering, too, by means of a gift of carrots or, less often, apples. Nonfood gifts, such as a drawing by the child, may also be left out for Santa. Children, informant interviews and field notes suggest, help to decide how this custom is implemented and may remind their parents about the Santa offertory. Thus children play an active role in maintaining and shaping this ritual:

> They [the children] always get out stuff for [Santa,] the cookies, hot chocolate, and carrots for the reindeer. [CDC: Where did that tradition come from?] Cookies were always from my family. I think the carrots must have been from [my husband's] family. And the kids decided on hot chocolate. I think we used to always have milk.

They get out the carrots. And he was awfully worried that there was six and not eight carrots [for the eight reindeer] [laughter]. I just bought a bunch, the kind with the green stuff at the end [laughter]. I didn't look at them. Well, [my son] was furious with me.

[My daughter] reminded us to put out the "cookies—no banana—for Santa." We always give him a banana because we figure he needs something healthy by this time.

Despite the fact that contemporary houses often have no chimneys, the assumption remains that Santa makes his entrance to the house by descending the chimney. This dictates that the offered food and drink for Santa be left near the hearth when possible. The chimney and hearth represent warmth and coziness, a protected inner sanctum and family gathering place ("home and hearth") into which Santa descends from above. As Eliade has observed, cosmological meanings and ritual functions are commonly associated with chimneys ("smoke holes"); the chimney recalls the rising smoke of a fire altar, which links a higher plane with a lower plane.[11] In the case of Christmas, the plane at the base of the chimney, the fireplace, is undisputably the domain of family life. The fireplace holds an important place within the family domain, the mantel being a place where family members display objects of importance in a "decorative shrine."[12] In turn, the chimney provides entrance into the hearth-centered domicile, an entrance at once magical and old-fashioned. Just as the fire provides a place to warm up on a cold day, so does Santa's arrival reinforce notions of warmth and human connectedness within the family setting. (The imagery of "chestnuts roasting on an open fire" and "stockings hung by the chimney with care" from Christmas songs encode a similar meaning.)

If Santa descends from a higher plane, this too is not surprising in view of his many godlike qualities, as kids understand them. As some children perceive, Santa's very entrance into the home is magical. As one five-year-old explained, for example, a potion could be involved: "Remember in Alice in Wonderland, when she drinks from that bottle, and she gets smaller? Santa could probably do that."

Like any dominant symbol—and Santa Claus is a dominant symbol in the American yuletide festival—Santa is full of varied meanings to children. First of all, Santa is fat, signifying (along with his hearty, jolly demeanor) indulgence, abundance, and bountifulness. Excessive eating (for that matter, excessive indulgence of all kinds) is part and parcel of the customary observation of Christmas and is emblematic within Santa's appearance. One young informant maintained that Santa could not diet, for "if he didn't eat that much, there would be no Santa"—that is, a skinny Santa would cease existence. In another youngster's perception, Santa Claus eats "a Thanksgiving feast every single day." Children seem to sense that Santa (and thereby Christmas) registers a level of indulgence far beyond that of everyday life. This, of course, is inherent to the nature of festival, as Roger Abrahams has aptly summarized.

> The vocabulary of festival is the language of extreme experiences through contrasts—contrasts between everyday life and these high times, and, within the events themselves, between the different parts of the occasion. . . . The performing self, too, is expected to be playfully distorted, for everyone involved is expected to eat or drink to excess. . . . All of these motives underscore the spirit of increase, of stretching life to the fullest, that lies at the heart of festive celebrations. The language of these celebrations of increase emerges from the everyday way of doing things, then, but alters them severely as it puts them into play and display.[13]

The excess of Christmas, eating, drinking, party going, and the large-scale giving of material gifts, has the paradoxical effect of causing festival participants (adults at least) to be glad to restore order and return to ordinary life afterward. There is an intensity to Christmas that cannot be sustained, as one mother explained.

> [Our Christmas tree and decorations] will come down New Year's Eve or New Year's Day, whenever we get a chance to. And that'll be it. Then it's over with. . . . Clean everything up and everything goes back to normal [laughter]. Isn't it terrible?

By the end of Christmas you just want it over with and get back to normal. And clean everything up.

Not only are the excesses of Christmas encoded in Santa's physical size, but perhaps, too, in his grandfatherly age, insofar as grandparents are widely equated with the unchecked indulgence of children. The contrasts Roger Abrahams expects within the components of festival events or symbols are exemplified by Santa's ancient age, in contrast to the newborn Jesus and to all children, who are the reason for the celebration.

Another contrast occurs in Santa's red attire, a prominent, lively, fiery, warm color, set in vivid opposition to the frigid, icy, white or gray, lifeless natural environment of the winter solstice. As Rudolph's red nose helps him to see through the fog, Santa visibly shows himself by wearing red. This is a form of revelation, by which the sacred reveals itself in startling ways to "the mental world of those who believe."[14] In other words, Santa's red suit conspicuously asserts the power of the spiritual or transcendent, making visible that which is so elusive. The red of a stop sign, stoplight, Red Cross logo, or fire engine is designed to attract attention. The same effect can also be applied to Santa's suit, as is clear when Mary (age seven) explains why Santa wears red, not green.

> I don't think green would look good on [Santa]. And red's a Christmas color, so I think that would be good. . . . But green, something about it, it just doesn't look good on him. . . . It doesn't look right [laughter]. Something about it. And he'd be bright red, and they'd be looking at him and saying, "Oh there he is!" But if he was green, he'd just be sort of sitting there. . . . So people can see him better. With the green, he'd just sort of sit there. But if he was red, people would just say, "There he is! Hi!"

An irony of Santa's prominent red suit is that so many of his other aspects signal that Santa is secret, remote, "invisible," "sneaky," and hidden. For one thing, Santa's nocturnal arrival (and the canon that "He won't come if you're not asleep") serves to impart a dreamlike mystery to his arrival. As Scott (age seven) explained:

[He comes] when everybody's asleep. He wants to stay a secret. He doesn't want anybody to see him. He wants everybody to be surprised on Christmas Day and see they got presents and Santa came. If he came in the daytime, everybody would know he came. . . . I think it's better at night. . . . There can be lots of surprises. . . . [I like things] sort of secret, and you have to figure out and use your noggin.

Stephanie, age nine, agreed that an element of invisibility, even spirituality, is involved in Santa's coming (though she assumes his entry is through the door, not the chimney).

He can walk right through. He's invisible, and he can walk right through like a ghost. He's the Christmas spirit.

Mothers agree that Santa's nocturnal arrival fits with Santa's elusive transcendence.

They say he comes to you only when you're sleeping. Probably because he is like . . . the idea of an elf or kind of like a dream. I suppose fairylike. Like something out of a storybook. Kind of a mystery person. That kind of an idea, that he's maybe a little unrealistic. Maybe that's why he comes at night. . . . And it's peaceful at night and quiet at night, and everything is calm, that might be why. It certainly seems like the best time to come.

He comes at night so nobody sees him. And if you see him, he disappears.

Santa's North Pole dwelling contributes to the sense that Santa is remote and secretive, being a desolate, secluded, unattainable, distant place. By living in the terrain of frozen ice and snow, Santa ensures that potential interlopers will be, in effect, snow-blind. In addition, the North Pole is perceived by children as a kind of winter wonderland, full of wondrous things such as "snowmen who can talk" and "reindeer who can fly."

CDC: I would like to pretend that we rode in a plane. . . . You tell me when we get to the North Pole.
MIKE (age seven): Now.

CDC: Okay, what do we see?

MIKE: Um, we see white.

CDC: White, what is it? A bride's dress, or what? What is all this white we see?

MIKE: Snow.

CDC: Snow. You mean Santa Claus lives where there's a lot of snow?

MIKE: Uh-huh.

CDC: Why would anyone want to do that?

MIKE: So nobody can find him.

Normal means of transportation would be inadequate to reach the North Pole, Ryan, age six, explained: "It's frozen there, and we can't make it with a car because the gas will go out very easy because it's so long away." Distance and snow give Santa an aura of seclusion and apartness.

Santa's wrapped gifts further the impression of a hidden "surprise" behind the veil of the immediately apparent. Ripping open the gifts constitutes an exciting revelation: Surprise at there being more than meets the eye is a pleasure in itself. "They should be wrapped. I like to be surprised" was a typical juvenile explanation for this sentiment. Maureen, age seven, concurred:

> I like it better if they're wrapped. . . . They surprise you more. It makes you surprised, and it makes you feel like "Oh! Oh!" [voice pitch raised, with excitement]. You just pull it apart. "Oh, look at this! Oh! Oh!" And you get real excited about it.

Folklorist Roger Abrahams has set forth the expressive argument (in one aspect, at least) implicit in the common decision to decoratively wrap.

> The language of holiday and festival maintains . . . a repertoire of symbolic images and movements in which the power of the most typical kinds of things may be condensed and then exploded, or cut up and dispersed; it is not simple chance that makes not only the parade but the lowly firecracker and the balloon, the wrapped present, the cornucopia, the pinata, the stuffed turkey, and Santa's stuffed bag the most powerful and pervasive images of our holidays. These embody the essence

of holiday wholeness on the one hand, then the breaking, cutting, exploding that allow everyone to share the now-freed energies and resources.[15]

Folklorists' theories aside, wrapping gifts is a time-consuming process with which some parents decide to dispense. In fact, whether or not to wrap can be a subject for husband-wife negotiation, an issue within the family ritual process. At times, the practical argument not to wrap the gifts wins out over the expressive contention that "tearing paper off" adds meaning to the ritual. Thus, despite the sentiment of one spouse ("It's fun to see the kids tear the paper off"), another spouse may prevail in some families ("Let's just set them out").

If Santa's remote residence, unseen nighttime arrival, and (at times) wrapped gifts are emblematic of being separate from empirical, visible reality, the implication that Santa belongs to a transcendent—perhaps supernatural—reality bears thought. Like belief in God, belief in Santa Claus amounts to an act of faith requiring a suspension of disbelief on the part of the believing subject. The analogy between God and Santa Claus is implicit to some parents' own observations of their children, like these recorded in one informant's field notes.

> Driving home from [my son's] violin lesson tonight. Dark outside. [My daughter] in front seat of van next to me. I said something about God—can't remember what although I remember following it up with a discourse on "God made the trees, the earth, the sun." "Did he make the signs?" [my daughter asked.] "No . . . he made the flowers." . . . [My daughter] said, "I don't believe in God and Santa Claus. How come they never die?"

To juvenile believers, Santa is not only immortal but omniscient, capable of supernatural ("magic") acts, and an enforcer of moral behavior. Such godlike qualities as omniscience are attributed to Santa in the context of children's daily behavior, as reported by mothers in field notes.

> [My son's] grandmother (who will be sleeping on the sofa bed in the living room, near the fireplace) said, "When Santa

comes, I'll close my eyes and pretend I'm sleeping." [My son]
said, "He can hear, you know," with a tone of voice clearly
condemning her pretense.

Watching TV, the 900 phone number for Santa came on. My
mom [the children's grandmother] was with [the children],
watching cartoons. [My son] said, "We don't need to call. Santa
*knows* what we want."

In an interview, another mother said,

We go to church, and he has CCD classes, which is catechism,
you know, religion classes. And they're taught that God sees
everything and he knows; he knows what you're doing and
when you're doing it. If you need help, he's there. And he
watches over you. And I think, what I was telling him about
Santa one time, about being good, Santa knows if you don't
behave. He kinda got the same feeling. "Oh well, Santa watches
over me all year round too." . . . He says, "Is he like God, does
he do the same thing God does?"

No matter who was conducting an interview (and seven different
investigators participated in this body of research), interviewers
found that children directly linked God and Santa Claus. Other
researchers have also found that children link Santa and God. In
a study by David Elkind on children's prayer, one five-year-old
girl defined a prayer as being "about God, rabbits, dogs, and
fairies and deer, and Santa Claus and turkeys and pheasants, and
Jesus and Mary and Mary's little baby."[16] Gordon Allport, in his
classic study *The Individual and His Religion,* observes that children
often "equate" Santa Claus and God.[17] Scheibe also found that it
was common for children to connect Santa Claus and God, as
illustrated by the following anecdote:

One father told of the son asking him if he was really Santa
Claus. The father had admitted that he was, after which the
boy thought for a while, and then asked if his father was also
the Tooth Fairy. Again the father admitted that he was. The
son then asked if the father was also the Easter Bunny, and
when the father said yes, the son asked "Are you God too?"[18]

From a child's perspective, the Santa legend is more than a legend. Santa is a spiritual reality that encourages their moral development ("He knows if you've been bad or good"), ensures them of a transcendent, higher being concerned with their mortal welfare ("He's up there watching me all the time"), to whom sacrificial offerings can be made (milk and cookies left at hearthside) and even "prayers" spoken ("You ask him for what you want, he can hear you"). No wonder, then, that children directly connect Santa Claus to God. For example:

[Boy, six:] God made [Santa Claus] magic.

[Boy, six:] He [God] lives next door [to Santa]. . . . I think they know each other. . . . Santa was flying, and God was outside watering his flowers if he has any [gleeful smile]. And then they started talking and got to be friends.

[Girl, six:] [Santa] know[s] that kids [have] been good or bad . . . because I think God tells him.

[Boy, seven:] God asked Santa Claus to bring presents. And God asked the Easter Bunny to bring eggs.

The childhood pantheon of Santa Claus, the Easter Bunny, and the Tooth Fairy bears connection, if not resemblance, to God. Yet when parents are aware that their children make this connection—especially parents who attend a fundamentalist Christian church—they are apt to be uncomfortable with the analogy. Mrs. Graham, herself raised in a fundamentalist church she still attended, now with her own children, had "mixed feelings" about the Santa Claus custom precisely because of the analogy between Santa Claus and God. (In my research, I have also met fundamentalist parents uncomfortable with the Tooth Fairy and the Easter Bunny, who are in their way of thinking "false idols" as well.)

Someone with all the godly qualities, actually a lot of the attributes of Santa, nobody really possesses them except God. So how can you . . . say someone has all the qualities. Like Santa, OK, he goes everywhere in one night. I mean, how could someone do that? . . . Who has the power to do that? And who has the power to know everything? Nobody has that power but God. And . . . you don't want to take away from the only person that has it is God and give it to someone, give it to supposedly a man. . . . And Santa'll give you everything. And God doesn't. So then, almost giving him all the best, best stuff. And God, he can be mean once in a while, and he can do bad things . . . to teach you a lesson.

Didactic attempts to avoid having Santa compete for attention with God were in evidence both in parochial schools and in the institutional policy of certain church groups, for example, Jehovah's Witnesses. Jessie (age seven) explained that she'd been taught in Catholic school that Santa, unlike Saint Nick (i.e., St. Nicholas, a religious saint whose feast day is celebrated by some families on December 6), is not holy.

From school they told us that Saint Nick and Santa are different. . . . When Santa was born, it was ho, ho, ho. When Saint Nick was born, it was holy, holy, holy.

Yet later in the same interview, this girl changed her mind and maintained that "Santa is holy and Catholic just like Saint Nick. Because he gives toys and he makes things for all the kids and people." Thus, the attempt to teach Jessie to draw a distinction between Santa and the holy Saint Nick was only partially successful.

The campaign on the part of the Jehovah's Witnesses to denigrate the Santa Claus custom long has been waged in the publication *Awake!*, as a passage from the December 22, 1955 issue demonstrates:

Throughout the year parents punish children for telling falsehoods. Yet parents abet the Santa Claus lie. Is it any wonder that many children, when they grow up and learn the truth, begin to believe God is a myth too? One little fellow, sadly disillusioned about Santa Claus, said to a playmate: "Yes, and I'm going to look into this 'Jesus Christ' business too!" Christmas is dangerously deceptive. It undermines Christianity and obscures the principles of true worship.

Yet the appetite of the juvenile mythological imagination is such that didactic attempts to eradicate Santa from children's minds are not uniformly successful. Children of fundamentalist Christian parents included in my research (with only one exception) insisted that Santa existed despite the influence of their churches and parents. Children also freely decided for themselves whether or not selected aspects of the myth were worthy of belief: A few kids rejected Rudolph as a "made-up story," even though most children believed in the ninth, red-nosed reindeer who guided Santa's sleigh. Perhaps it is not surprising that "works of the religious imagination, whose function is to communicate meaning through symbolic form rather than to copy external facts,"[19] should adopt idiosyncratic form for each individual. Rather than directly copying the model of others (either other children, parents, or religious teachers), children incorporate the myth in their own way. For a myth to maintain meaning, the individual must actively accept the myth as vital. The question of whether Santa Claus is true or false is poorly phrased, in the final analysis, since it implies a static, unchanging basis for mythological reality. The reality of Santa Claus is contingent upon the believing subject's acceptance. And acceptance is up to the child—or, perhaps, the believing adult. (A few adults insisted that they still believed in Santa Claus, albeit in a "spiritual" sense.)

Neither God nor Santa Claus are entities that can be "thought out," strictly speaking. They belong to the realm of dreamlike mystery and numinous experience, given how children (and adults) experience them. It comes as a revelation of this ethnographic research that social scientists or parents who treat children's belief in Santa Claus as an instance of immature reasoning about real and make-believe have missed something important: Faith, not reasoned skepticism, is the relevant mental experience. Santa Claus gives young children an experience in which the value of faith is endorsed by most adults, from editors who write confirming "Yes, Virginia" essays to creators of affirming movies such as *Miracle on 34th Street*. Once a year at least, among young children at least, faith prevails in the modern Western world.

Of course, children do eventually give up their literal belief in Santa Claus. But, apparently, children's capacity for faith in a higher, transcendent reality (perhaps a less literally presented one) is not lost just because Santa Claus proves mortal. As eight-year-old Peter mused:

> Some people think it's not real . . . Santa Claus. Some people at the North Pole walked around it, and they say that Santa Claus isn't there. They looked everywhere. Scientists. When the presents are there on Christmas, I don't know where he is. . . . They looked every inch of the Arctic, . . . I saw it in some of the books. . . . Probably it's God doing all this stuff, and it's Santa Claus who's not real.

Moreover, an abstract understanding of Santa's reality is typically retained by children after literal belief in Santa is lost. For instance, in Peter's case (now at age nine), this involved an external source, unseen but generous:

> [When I was five,] I heard no bells, I heard no reindeer. I heard no "Ho, ho, ho." I didn't hear anything. . . . I *really* thought there *was* a Santa Claus. . . . When I growed up, it just started to sort of slip away and I forgot about it, like fading, fading away. . . . [Now] I still a little bit believe in Santa Claus. . . . It's like he's down there and I can't see him . . . and he's like giving me something very special.

In Rachel's case, at age nine the abstract remnants of her Santa Claus belief were more internalized:

> There isn't a person who lives at the North Pole with little elves helping him. . . . But there's a feeling inside you at Christmastime which makes you feel good and happy and everything.

If children's voices are taken to heart, Santa Claus is anything but a threat to children's generalized capacity for faith. Imaginal experience is not single-minded and exclusive so much as open-minded and organic. That is, a child can lose literal belief in Santa but retain the visionary powers to believe in whatever still provides sanctuary and meaning. The human capacity for faith seems able to transcend a loss of the concrete meaning of a symbol. Faith is a never ending story, able to endure in less concrete, culturally mature forms.

# *Five*

# Journey down the Bunny Trail:
# *Easter Bunny and Easter*

*Omne vivum ex ovo* (all life comes from an egg).
—Latin proverb

It may seem a short, springy step from Santa to the Easter Bunny (from ho ho ho to hop hop hop, as it were), but it would be a mistake to equate these imaginal figures. For one thing, Christmas and Easter represent opposed holidays. This has been suggested in the writings of Caplow and his collaborators from the famed Middletown study.[1] My own work with families suggests that Christmas and Easter oppose one another on a fundamental level indeed. Christmas occurs at a bleak, lightless, deadened time of year. Devoid of natural sources of enjoyment, festival participants import (from the equally lifeless climate of the North Pole) a celebration that is manufactured and culturally, not naturally, derived. The cultural rootedness of the yuletide holiday, symbolized by Santa's factory, is made inevitable by climactic bleakness. Snow and the fir tree (for which, at any rate, many celebrants substitute a man-made counterfeit) aside, the rituals largely depend on manufactured devices (toys, chimney, sleigh) or domesticated forms (reindeer) rather than untamed, natural emblems. The chaos and uncontrollability of nature is not a theme given prominence at Christmas. If snow is depicted in Christmas decorations, it is picturesque, the idealized "white Christmas," and not stormlike. Santa, a brightly suited human, is the dominant icon, aligned with culture, not nature.

By contrast, Easter is a time of natural brilliance: bright light, colorful vegetation, emerging warmth, animal propagation. With all the beauty and enjoyment provided by nature, there is no need to further gild the lily. Nature itself provides the key emblems and festival material. First, there is a rabbit, the Easter Bunny, who, children agree, is white rather than brightly colored (brightness being superfluous, perhaps, since nature itself is so full of color) and who lives in a natural setting, in the forest, perhaps underground in a cavelike warren. Second, there are the baskets: woven of natural materials (and rustic in their associations) and filled with natural contents. Among these contents might be found animal- or egg-shaped candies, "grass" (which is ubiquitous in its use, and ubiquitous also in its tendency to spread all over the household), and eggs, derived from nature and requiring gentle treatment from human hands when dyed, so as not to break this natural object. When a toy is given in the basket, often it is to be used in outdoor play: kites, jump ropes, beach pails, toy lawn mowers or wheelbarrows, sidewalk chalk, or even (in one case) a bicycle.

In short, Easter contrasts with Christmas at the most fundamental level, as nature contrasts with culture. People celebrate at Christmas despite the hardships of cold, dark nature—indeed to escape, overcome, and assert control over those hardships. At Easter, people celebrate because the natural splendor of the vernal equinox calls for a seasonal rite of passage to welcome spring.

Natural energies, Sherry Ortner has asserted, are associated with the physiology of procreation (and therefore with women)—a systematic relationship that also involves an association between nature and children. Just as Easter is aligned with nature, so too are children.[2]

One can easily see how infants and children might themselves be considered part of nature. Infants are barely human and utterly unsocialized; like animals they are unable to walk upright, they excrete without control, they do not speak. Even slightly older children are clearly not yet fully under the sway of culture. They do not yet fully understand social duties, responsibilities and morals; their vocabulary and range of learned skills are small. . . . Most cultures have initiation rites for adolescents . . . the point of which is to move the child ritually from a less than fully human state into full participation in society and culture. . . . Thus children are likely to be categorized with nature, and woman's close association with children may compound her potential for being seen as closer to nature herself.

Christmas, whose principal icon is an emphatically mature male, is aligned with culture. It is thus not surprising to find (as we did in the prior chapter) that Christmas is not in fact a holiday for children, despite native insistence to the contrary. Easter, however, is decidedly a child-oriented festival, as this chapter will demonstrate. Children play an especially active role in maintaining and shaping the rituals of Easter. The primal, preverbal nature of the festival's chief icon, the huggable, mute Easter Bunny whose gifts are orally gratifying, appeals to the young far more than to adults. The child-directed tradition of Easter does not support or connect with the adult mythology of Easter, the Resurrection narrative. (By contrast, as will be discussed in the next chapter, children consciously make a connection between the religious story of the infant Jesus and the beneficence of Santa Claus.) Easter—as a celebration of new life, uncontrollable though that natural process may sometimes be—is consonant with children's own station as newly living and thus a holiday at one with juvenile experience.

Mrs. Joseph, mother of six-year-old Brian and eight-year-old Lisa, typifies the almost blasé attitude of mothers toward preparations for children's Easter rituals. Her daughter spurred her into action when it came to Easter decorations.

> This year my daughter decorated the house. She was the one who said, "When can we get the Easter stuff down?" And my husband got it down for her. And she said, "Can I decorate?" And I said, "That's fine."

Mrs. Joseph was equally nonchalant about organizing an Easter egg hunt. She explained that the children's grandfather took care of that, and if he didn't do it, she was sure her sister would. Yet Mrs. Joseph had an entirely different approach to Christmas, which she began to actively discuss and prepare for as early as October. "Christmas," in her mind, "always seemed to be a bigger deal." By contrast, she said, "I could give up Easter. It could be a regular Sunday. That would be okay."

Mrs. Joseph's young son Brian was not nearly so uninterested in Easter rituals. He smiled as he told me about the "fun" of finding a purple egg "hiding in a little tree" at his cousin's house. Nor did he dismiss the "Bunny that hops around the whole wide world to give children candy." Of course, candy is something only children are interested in, he implied—when explaining that the Easter Bunny would not leave *me* any. "Grown-ups don't eat candy," he asserted. I might expect to receive a "bonnet," he guessed, but never candy.

In this typical family, Easter is a holiday where children actively carry on the celebration. Adults go along with the children's initiatives, but they themselves are relatively passive.

## VISITING THE EASTER BUNNY

In my fieldwork, the difference between Christmas and Easter was nowhere more keen than at the shopping mall where I observed children visiting the Easter Bunny and Santa. First, the bright natural light (emanating from a skylight) at Easter season cast a dazzling illumination, against which the dim light at Christmastime paled by comparison. Amid this natural glow, the Easter Bunny impersonator occupied a setting that was itself a study in contrasts: Rather than a thronelike chair surrounded by larger-than-life toys as for Santa, the Easter Bunny occupied a bench placed in front of the trunk of a large tree within which "the Easter Bunny lives," one child was heard to say. The remaining decor consisted of nature-derived flora and fauna, including a fenced-in display of living animals (baby ducks and three rabbits), which children could pet and hold.

Children did not appear to shy away from the animals in the display, either the living animals or the Easter Bunny impersonator. Parents seldom forced (or needed to force) the issue when it came to having children pose with the Easter Bunny for a photo. On those few occasions where youngsters hesitated, they were removed from the Easter Bunny's lap before crying. Only one child (a three-month-old infant) was observed to cry at all while visiting the Easter Bunny.

This virtual lack of crying differs markedly from the behavior shown while visiting Santa Claus, on whose lap tearful children were repeatedly coaxed to stay by parents. Sometimes, children were photographed visiting Santa despite their weeping discomfort. On balance, visiting Santa Claus was an adult-driven event, whereas visiting the Easter Bunny was child driven. Children were apt to run and hug the Easter Bunny without prodding. Indeed, some children remained with the Easter Bunny despite their parents' eagerness to have them depart. One videotaped observation yielded the following transcript.

> Child, a two-year-old boy, walks over to Bunny unescorted and extends arms to Bunny. Bunny tousles boy's hair. Boy hugs Bunny. Bunny lifts child up to lap. Child is smiling.
>
> MOTHER: Are you ready, are you done? Come on, let's go. Come on. Now come on. Say good-bye to the Easter Bunny. Tell him to bring you lots of goodies.

Children's eagerness and independent desire to be with the Easter Bunny was described in the journal of one Easter Bunny impersonator, who recorded that children ages three to seven "ran to me, hugged me, and even kissed my false face."[3] So, too, did the children I observed run up and hug the Bunny without parental encouragement. Two brothers ran from their mother some distance away to the Bunny, an act about which the mother became quite angry. Talking with her, I learned that she was a Jehovah's Witness opposed to the custom that her sons were eager to embrace—literally. She worried about her status with her fellow Jehovah's Witnesses if it became known that her sons associated with the Bunny. (She asked me not to use the word "Easter" in referring to the Bunny.)

Children, when interviewed, did not think that the impersonator looked like the real Easter Bunny. The real Bunny would be less humanlike in size and posture. But nevertheless, their encounter with the shopping mall rabbit was said to be comfort giving, much like a "furry pillow." As Andy (age six) said:

> It was furry. . . . You get to put your hand on him. It'll feel
> furry, real furry. And when you don't have any pillow, you
> lost it, then you could put your head on this.

Undoubtedly, the fact that the Easter Bunny impersonator was speechless gave young children a more equal footing in the interaction than is the case with Santa Claus, since their own budding capacities for speech were untaxed. Rather than interacting verbally, kids were apt to walk right over to the Bunny and pull, tug, or hug. The video camera operator wondered if children thought the Bunny was a stuffed animal, since they treated it with such free willingness to pat, poke, and stroke. Interaction between child and Bunny was consistently physical and primal: hugs, hand play, pats, peekaboo, knee bouncing, hand holding, waving, kiss blowing, swaying, tickling. The Bunny impersonator had coloring books to offer the child, another nonverbal gesture. Sometimes the Bunny pointed out the basket of coloring books and gestured for the child to take one; at other times the accompanying photographer gave the child a book. But the coloring books were often forgotten. Children were happy to "play" physically with the Easter Bunny or to exchange affectionate hugs and pats. My informants endorsed the view that the Easter Bunny is comparable to a "pet" that "you can pick up" and cuddle.

The ease with which the costumed Bunny became an object of comfort and affection suggests that, in some respects, the Easter Bunny impersonator was treated as a transitional object. A transitional object corresponds to a child's blanket, teddy bear, or other "not-me" possession that is affectionately cuddled, used as a defense against anxiety and as an aid to sleeping, and relied upon in times of stress.[4] While the Easter Bunny impersonator did not fulfill all these roles, it was indeed treated much as a transitional object might be hugged and stroked.

Intriguingly, one informant, Mrs. Stewall, reported that her five-year-old's transitional object was none other than a stuffed bunny.

> My five-year-old has got a bunny and Bunny goes with him
> whenever things get stressful. Bunny appeared wearing a hos-

pital gown in surgery. . . . He went to the hospital with him [when he had his tonsils out]. . . . And he went to the hospital when he had his hernia removed. He went to the first day of preschool. He had to take him for his very first show-and-tell. . . . So for my five-year-old, Bunny is a real important figure in his life. . . . So it's real easy for the tradition of a bunny doing something like [the Easter Bunny] does, it's really easily explained to the imagination of the young child.

A rabbit, this mother reasoned, was an ideal species for transitional objecthood, since "He makes no noises, [and] they use their imaginations and the bunny can be or say or do whatever they want him to be." This is precisely the impression that arose from observing children, even very young children, cuddle and fondle the Easter Bunny impersonator.

As empirically oriented as American culture may be, there is nevertheless some rein given to imaginal thinking, which goes beyond the sensible, material, externalized reality to include "the intermediate area between the subjective and that which is objectively perceived."[5] Judging from stories within American popular culture, one nexus for imaginal activity lies in narratives involving rabbits. For instance, consider the widely known story of the Velveteen Rabbit. This story, received by one young informant as a gift in her Easter basket, is a variation on a common motif in children's literature, the toy that comes alive. The Velveteen Rabbit is a stuffed animal so loved by its juvenile owner as to become real and to live among woodland, animate rabbits.

Shared fantasies about bunnies have been reported in the literature on family ritual. As a case in point, one father and daughter made up legends about "Bunyan Bunny," a large "superbunny" who caused the formation of Niagara Falls by slipping while getting a drink from a spring. Father and daughter called their partnership the "rabbit club," under the auspices of which they wove rich fantasies about Bunyan Bunny.[6]

Another well-known instance of an imaginal bunny is the play and movie *Harvey,* by Mary Chase, in which the adult character Elwood meets a white rabbit that only believers are capable of seeing. As Elwood describes meeting Harvey:

I started to walk down the street when I heard a voice saying: "Good evening, Mr. Dowd." I turned, and there was this great white rabbit leaning against a lamp-post. Well, I thought nothing of that, because when you have lived in a town as long as I have lived in this one, you get used to the fact that everybody knows your name. Naturally, I went over to chat with him. . . . We stood there and talked, and finally I said—"You have the advantage of me. You know my name and I don't know yours." Right back at me he said: "What name do you like?" Well, I didn't even have to think a minute: Harvey has always been my favorite name. So I said, "Harvey," and this is the interesting part of the whole thing. He said—"What a coincidence! My name happens to be Harvey."[7]

Bunyan Bunny, the Velveteen Rabbit, and Harvey share the qualities of transitional objects, in that the participation of the subject, the perceiver, is decisive in creatively making contact with the object. That is, a boy's love makes a stuffed rabbit come alive; or a man's idealized property—being named Harvey—is brought out in the transitional object. This experiencing involves the creative inner life of the individual interacting with the symbolic world. But this is not to say that a hallucination is involved. The transitional object is neither external to, nor internally conceived by, the individual. The paradox is left unresolved, and the object is said to exist in transitional space.

American popular culture seemingly allows rabbits to be perceived as transitional objects, in this paradoxical (some might say magical) way. Recall that rabbits are thought to be drawn out of hats by magicians, to have feet that can be transformed into lucky charms, and to descend into magical rabbit holes, as in Lewis Carroll's stories of Alice.[8]

Moreover, bunnies are "cute" animals, associated with fertility (pregnancy tests, and numerous offspring) and with infancy and early childhood, that early developmental stage which might be thought of as the "nursery" period. As already discussed, early childhood is a time associated with the capacity for imagination and suspended disbelief. Baby merchandise and clothing in America are often decorated with bunnies, including Beatrix Potter's illustrations of Peter Rabbit, or Bunnykins illustrations on Royal Doulton pottery. Bunnies are suitable Halloween costumes for children under six but thought too babyish for older children.[9]

If bunnies are associated with young children, and in turn are associated with imaginal perception as transitional objects, no wonder that children who visit the Easter Bunny impersonator embrace this soft, furry creature so readily. An Easter Bunny impersonator reported that he came to expect kids to express affection and "began to measure his days in the number of waves and hugs received."[10] Likewise, the costumed Easter Bunny at a shopping mall which I visited (a woman, with whom I became friendly enough to go in the "back room" while she removed her outer costume to cool off) expressed deep sadness at making the transition to being a "normal person" (not the Easter Bunny) and losing the hugs and affection to which she had become accustomed. The Easter Bunny is a more approachable figure than Santa Claus from a child's perspective, all evidence shows. Conversely, from an adult perspective, encouraging a child to approach the Easter Bunny is not really necessary and also not worth exertion of effort. It is the child, not the adult, who most actively shapes the custom of visiting the nonverbal, nature-associated Easter Bunny. This observation is indirectly substantiated by Norman Prentice, Martin Manosevitz, and Laura Hubbs, who found that "parents are not as involved in the Easter Bunny myth as they are with Santa Claus."[11]

## THE EASTER BUNNY: (SUPER)NATURAL ICON

American folklore and popular culture abound with rabbit figures who take on anthropomorphic qualities: Bugs Bunny, Brer Rabbit, the movie character Roger Rabbit, Peter Rabbit—not to mention the bow tie–wearing Playboy trademark. Yet the Easter Bunny is not a humanlike personification, as children describe him. (The male pronoun will be used in reference to the Bunny, since the Easter Bunny was often, though not always, said to be male.) On the contrary, the Easter Bunny is totemic, that is, animallike. First of all, just like the Easter Bunny impersonator at the shopping mall, the real Easter Bunny does not talk, according to juvenile consensus. Additionally, children affirm that he by and large does not wear human clothes (despite illustrations by adult artists that often depict the Bunny with clothing). Further, the Bunny hops rather than walks upright. Children were so convinced of this that they themselves tended to hop up and down while role-playing the Easter Bunny. As an offering of food for the Easter Bunny, children left carrots (a raw food "that animals would eat") rather than a prepared food such as cookies. Finally, the Easter Bunny lacks a name, unlike a domesticated pet or a personified bunny such as Peter Rabbit or Bugs Bunny.

Overall, the contrast between the Easter Bunny and a personified rabbit (such as the popular media figures Roger Rabbit or Bugs Bunny) was marked. Tom, age six, reasoned as follows:

> [Roger Rabbit] doesn't act like the Easter Bunny. . . . The Easter Bunny doesn't talk, and he talks. And the Easter Bunny doesn't kiss, and he does. And the Easter Bunny doesn't have a bow on, I mean a tie. . . . The Easter Bunny hops and [Bugs Bunny] walks. . . . [Bugs Bunny] wears gloves, and the Easter Bunny doesn't.

Peter Rabbit, too, was contrasted by children with the Easter Bunny, since Peter Rabbit was subject to the human foibles of "taking from other people's gardens."[12] In comparison, the Easter Bunny is morally upright and generous, one who rewards good children by leaving them an Easter basket.

The Easter Bunny was said to live in a rustic, natural setting, where trees and grass grow (a primeval woodland comparable to the setting for the movie *Bambi*), and perhaps where vegetables also grow. Amidst this growth-filled environment, the Easter Bunny was repeatedly described as living in an underground war-ren (a "cave," a "hole"). The Bunny's subterranean, underworld home ensures that he remains apart from the ordinary world ("no one can find him there"). Both the Easter Bunny and Santa Claus occupy cosmic domains apart from ordinary social space. But notably, the two holiday figures dwell in realms that are directly opposed, Santa living "up" and the Easter Bunny living "down."

Both an upper realm and an underworld are thus valid conceptions of sacred space to children, just as Eliade suggests for adult mythology.[13]

If the Easter Bunny represents primeval nature in his animal-like behavior and earthly domain, recall that his interaction with children (as embodied in the shopping mall impersonator) is also primal and free of language and, in that sense, unacculturated. Child informants described the Easter Bunny as "cute," "cuddly," "soft," "like a teddy bear," "a white fluffy little thing." The comforting, affectionate feelings (in native slang, "warm fuzzys") evoked by the Easter Bunny was compared by one mother to the comfort obtained from religion.

> Rabbits are so cute. Rabbits are so soft and furry. And they have those big floppy ears. . . . Cuddly little things . . . It's that warmth. I'm going to relate it back to church, because it's that warm inner feeling that you get, to know that it's Easter Sunday and the Resurrection and all that kind of good stuff. Stuffed animals are warm and cuddly. And through troubled times or through sad times, they provide some comfort and some security.

Native experience with the Easter Bunny thus lends support to Winnicott's contention that transitional space—an intermediate space neither subjective nor objective, in which the transitional object exists—expands with maturity to include adult religious and cultural experience.[14]

To the degree that the Easter Bunny involves a cognitive dimension (the capacity to suspend disbelief) necessary to the mythic imagination and an affective dimension (a sense of comfort, of emotional sanctuary) common to transitional phenomena, the Easter Bunny is an exemplar of the components of religious experience translated to the most primal level. Just as for Santa Claus, children at times insisted that the Easter Bunny was associated with God or with saints.

> [Boy, six:] [The Easter Bunny], he's like a spirit . . . something like, like God is a spirit.

[Girl, seven:] [He lives] with God.

[Girl, seven:] [He] knows Saint Nick, Saint Patrick, Santa Claus.

The Easter Bunny was also said by young informants to have supernatural qualities: magical abilities, including omniscience; immortality, though he is perceived as young in chronological age; and, especially, a sort of transcendence. The Easter Bunny is silent, shy, hidden, able to disappear at will or to hop very fast so as to avoid detection by ordinary eyes. Such qualities suggest that the Bunny is not a fixed, material being in the ordinary sense. As Mrs. Wattums expressed it, the Easter Bunny is "spiritual."

> When the Bunny comes to our house, it's spiritual. 'Cause you can't see the Bunny. And the Bunny won't come unless you're sleeping. . . . I don't know what they think of the Bunny as looking like. So I just think of it as spiritual, because how can you think of a real little bunny this big [gestures to show size of actual rabbit] carrying all these things around to everybody's house. It doesn't make sense. . . . Everything doesn't have to be seein' and touchin' it. There are some things in life, such as God, that they're not gonna see and touch. . . . They go to the store and they see the Bunny and they sit on his lap. Because maybe that's what brings it, the realness to it. And yet when they go to sleep, they can't see the Bunny. But that's OK, that's all right. At church there'll be people dressed up in costumes, and they know that's not really St. Nicholas or whoever, but they'll go along with it.

Another mother, Mrs. Wayne, emphasized the importance of distinguishing the concrete symbol of the Easter Bunny from the transcendent meaning it represents.

> I feel personally that you can know something is a fantasy or a story, like Santa Claus and the Easter Bunny, and yet still believe in the symbolism of it and what it's supposed to symbolize at the same time. . . . The spirit, the feeling, the love behind the whole thing and everything, that's what's real. And that's what I think the kids have to learn to distinguish.

Children can stop believing in the literal, concrete symbol, then, yet retain belief in "what it's supposed to symbolize." It is this paradox—that the transcendent meaning of a symbol can remain real long after the symbol's literal reality is dismissed—that is the developmental gift of imaginal holiday beings.

Curiously, despite the lack of material contact with the actual Easter Bunny, children now and then reported that they had witnessed evidence of his reality. Juvenile seers in a few cases had visions of the Easter Bunny directly. Mike, age seven, told his mother about his visionary experience.

> When you talk to my son, if you told him straight out, there really is no Easter Bunny, he'll say, "No, you're wrong. Because I've seen him." . . . Two years ago we stayed at my mom's [house]. . . . And he said, "You're not going to believe this. I saw the Easter Bunny." And the story gets bigger and bigger. He keeps making it more [elaborate]. He goes, "And then he turned around and waved to me and walked out the door." And then one time he was telling the story, and he said, "You know I thought I saw . . . a zipper at the back of his neck." . . . He saw it. It was there. I can't wait till you talk to him.

Mike was more conservative in the rendition told to me than his mother had predicted:

> We tried to see the Easter Bunny. We tried to see him this year. I saw him last year. . . . I just woke up and I was watching downstairs and I saw this giant rabbit. . . . I'm like, "Oh my God!" And then I was looking, and then I turned my head, and I looked in the other room, and then I looked again and he disappeared. . . . [CDC: Who do you think the rabbit was?] The Easter Bunny.

Young Mike made it clear that while his vision bore witness to the Easter Bunny's reality, the Bunny seldom made himself visible to children in this way.

Other children reported that footprints were left on the Easter basket or left "all over." (These footprints were not the doing of a parent, either, as separate interviews confirmed.) As one believer, age six, reported:

> We usually searched around for [the Easter Bunny] to see if
> he's still there. [Delighted expression on face:] Sometimes I
> find white footprints all over. . . . They were coming out the
> door all the way over to there. And about all around the house.

A girl, age seven, also saw footprints.

> I really think it's a Bunny [that comes] because every Easter I
> check at midnight to see if my mom and dad are up. Because
> that's when they get up. They told us last year, don't do it.
> But I check every time to make sure. They're always in bed.
> . . . [Last year] I could tell [the Easter Bunny came] because
> when I woke up I saw footprints . . . by my basket. . . . My
> mom threw my basket out because it got covered with foot-
> prints. Every year I got footprints.

Ultimately, it is important to respect the imaginal properties of
children's relating to the Easter Bunny. As Marion Milner has
said, transitional phenomena involve a two-way journey, "Both
to the finding of the objective reality of the object and to finding
the objective reality of the subject."[15] Milner agrees with Winnicott that the child's special toy, understood in this way as a
transitional entity coming neither from inside nor from outside
the child, "bridges" to the cultural field of religion as the child
develops. An important girder in this bridge is the Easter Bunny,
who with minimal parental encouragement both energizes children's faith and is energized by it.


## THE EASTER EGG HUNT

During the period when one mother was keeping field notes, her
seven-year-old daughter was given a school assignment to write
a haiku. She chose to write about Easter.

> Easter
> Green, colorful
> Hunting, eating, breaking
> We hunt for eggs holiday.

Her poem reflects what informants' commentary directly testifies: Hunting for eggs (as well as coloring them) is an important part of Easter to children, often the favorite part. When asked "What happened at Easter at your house?" children commonly summed up their activities by explaining, "We hunted for eggs." At times, the hunt was for hard-boiled eggs, which children had colored themselves, and which the Easter Bunny allegedly hid during the night. At other times, the hunt was for plastic eggs containing money, small toys, or candy. In some households, the egg hunt was known to have been staged by the parents, who gave clues about the whereabouts of the eggs ("you're warm," "you're cold"). Often, the eggs were coded according to the ability of children, with the eggs for younger children hidden in easier-to-find places. Or, perhaps, more clues were given to younger searchers to help them. Sometimes, eggs were labeled with a child's name, who was expected to find that egg.

One youngster compared hunting for eggs to a "treasure hunt"—although the thrill was attached to the process of hunting and finding more than the ultimate prize. Like hide-and-seek, hunting for eggs provides the pleasant anticipation of searching and the pleasurable excitement of finding, a happy moment that, according to one mother, makes youngsters "light up." And this process occurs within bounds of challenge well matched to a child's ability, so as to allow a sense of accomplishment without frustration. In short, hunting for eggs has the qualities of "flow" activity, providing the optimal state of involvement, without boring children or making them anxious.[16] Elements of randomness (where the eggs are hidden) combine with personal effort to determine the outcome. Mrs. Block's memory of her own childhood ritual recalls the fun involved when the luck of the draw combined with individual initiative.

When I grew up, my grandmother always folded change—pennies and nickels and dimes and quarters and dollar bills, she'd fold up . . . and [she] wrapped them in foil. And then when we went on our Easter egg hunts, you never knew, I mean it wasn't like she gave all the kids one dollar, in each egg or whatever. You had to hunt. It's just the luck of the draw, in what you got. And then we'd collect all of our own money and count it up. . . . It was fun.

A family egg hunt provides an outlet for sibling rivalry; that is, here the competition between siblings is formalized and given sanction, within certain limits. Children take pride in being able to say, "I found all my brother's [eggs]" or "My sister sleeps late, so I found most of them."

Public institutions also stage Easter egg hunts. Community park districts can take differing approaches to such an event. One approach, described by Mrs. Lohr, failed in her eyes because of its public display of excessive greed:

> There was an Easter egg hunt—actually they called it that, but all they do is throw out candy—at the park district. We've gone to two in the past two years. And I thought, that's really dumb. I grew up in a community, and they hid eggs, real eggs, and they dyed real eggs and hid them and it was just wonderful. There had to be two hundred kids there [at this one], and throwing candy in the grass and having kids scramble after. It was ridiculous, so I didn't tell [the children] about it this year.

This egg hunt failed to meet the implicit rules of authenticity: not just that real eggs were hunted for, but that the eggs were hidden and required some effort to find. Similarly, Mrs. Craven was invited to her brother's community for an Easter egg hunt sponsored by a fraternal society. This hunt also fell short of her own ideal type.

> It started at ten, and it was completely over at ten after ten. They just threw all this candy and some plastic eggs out in this field. . . . The preschoolers were in this field, the five-to-seven-year-olds, and then, I don't know what the other age was. But they said, "Go!" and the kids scattered, and if they found a plastic egg, they took it to the Easter Bunny and they got to pick a toy out of the basket. . . . It was a waste. It was a greedy little waste. . . . My niece . . . got, picked up, one piece of candy and that's it. [My daughter] got, like, two pieces of candy and found a plastic egg, so she thought she was done.

. . . These other kids out there were like out for blood. . . .
These kids had shopping bags full of this candy. And that just
seems kind of greedy, you know what I mean.

The Easter egg hunt, on a community level, becomes a metaphor
for the fair distribution of resources. To be fair, the outcome
should require effort, a search for hidden eggs, not an all-out
grab contest. The process should make allowances for the differing abilities of differing age groups. And the point should not
be to obtain as much treasure as possible, but rather to enjoy the
process of searching itself. Greed, in the form of ravaging the
environment for as much material gain as possible, is pointed up
as undesirable.

My own observation of an Easter egg hunt staged by a grocery
store further reveals the resource allocation metaphor inherent in
the hunt. At this grocery store, plastic eggs filled with candy or
coupons for prizes were hidden amid the merchandise in the
aisles. Children were organized such that those kids searching
each aisle were all the same age. In one aisle, the first boy in line
started to take the eggs at the beginning of the aisle. The kids
behind him searched in the same general area, getting the eggs
just beyond him. But one bright girl right at the outset went to
the very end of the aisle, where there were no other kids hunting.
She got twice as many eggs as the first boy. Another girl got no
eggs, but the manager handed her one when he saw her just
standing, not joining the fray. The analogy to the larger society,
where the financial gains come from going where the crowd isn't,
and where some need welfare, is tempting.

At another Park District egg hunt that I observed, egg hunters
were all the same age. The rule announced at the outset was "No
pushing and shoving, there's plenty for everybody." Children had
to search under obstacles, such as wishing wells, for the plastic
eggs and prizes. Mothers praised this hunt as "a little bit more
individual and searching," in that "you have your own path, and
you search what is right."

If mothers wish the Easter egg hunt to encode more than a
minimally involving scramble for wealth—they prefer, at best, an
active search for one's "own path"—it makes sense that the cus-

tom of coloring Easter eggs is widely practiced by families. When children color eggs, they derive a sense of personal control and active participation, since it is the child who typically does the dye work. A sense of self-expression by means of colorful transformation seems to lie behind all the fun. To quote two seven-year-old girls:

> [The Easter Bunny] makes us color your own eggs, and you get to do whatever choices you want. Half of green, yellow, red, pink, blue . . . and all kinds of different colors.

> [In an excited voice:] Do you know what? We had to put two spoons of vinegar, and then we had to put the colors in. And then we had to put the water in and stir it up and put our eggs in. And do you know what? I mixed some of the colors and made it brown. And do you know what? I made a pink egg, a blue egg, a green and white egg that are mixed together.

Mothers repeatedly admitted that their children provided momentum for the custom of dying eggs. Children many times instigate the ritual and remind the mother to do it. Further, children serve as the chief justification for maintaining the custom, which otherwise would be dropped. Youngsters enjoy coloring eggs so much that mothers put up with the mess despite their relative lack of personal motivation. As women explained in interviews:

> I wouldn't get away with [not dying eggs]. They wouldn't let me get away with it. They wouldn't even let me get away with, I tried one year . . . getting the little plastic eggs, putting the candy inside, and hiding them. They don't work with them. They have to be real eggs. They have to be boiled, they have to be dyed.

> Maybe they feel that it's their contribution to Easter, to the holiday. We [mothers] have a tendency to get wrapped up in cooking and cleaning and other things. And the kids [remind us]. . . . [My son] was big this year on eggs. "Why aren't we coloring them on Good Friday? We always color them on Good Friday." . . . I think in the coloring of the eggs, [it] gives them [an idea] that they're helping, they're doing something about Easter.

Let's put it this way. When they get to the age that they're no longer interested in doing it, I will not do it. I wouldn't do it for myself. . . . Even though I did it as a child. . . . I just do it for the kids. In fact, when [my son] was little, the first couple years before he was aware what was going on, we didn't color eggs. We didn't color them until he was old enough, and he was in preschool, where he found out that other people colored eggs. And that's how we started to color eggs.

Children, then, are the active force in maintaining the custom of coloring eggs. They do this not because they enjoy eating them. In fact, indications are that eggs are sometimes discarded rather than eaten completely. Nor did children care if the eggs were baked into bread, the ethnic custom in two families, or blessed at church, the custom among some Catholics. Rather, dying eggs was an enjoyable end in itself. Perhaps the equation of an egg with new life and new beginnings, of which adults are certainly aware, fits equally well with the interests of children, who enjoy creating something new and vivid. Children embody the life-affirming values of Easter within the essence of who they are: beings who are growing, who want to create colorful forms of self-expression (even if to do so is messy), who find searching for unfound treasure to be desirable and exciting.

To children, an egg is an object that is peeled to find something interesting within or that hatches to reveal a chick inside. As juvenile informants explained:

[Boy, age six, speaking in role of Easter Bunny:] Chicks come out of the eggs I bring.

[Girl, age seven:] [An egg] is something that birds come out of, or chicks, animals come out of.

[Girl, age seven:] You have to boil the egg, not just leave it raw. 'Cause [if you don't] a chick might hatch.

An egg, then, reveals a veiled mystery (much as the Easter egg hunt) and contains new life. Eggs are so special, indeed, that young informants sometimes felt that the Easter Bunny obtained eggs by means of magic: either through a magical chicken or through his own making.

In some instances, children decided to leave an offering of their own colored egg for the Easter Bunny. One mother reported in her field notes that this was a sufficiently important act to her daughter (age eight) that when her egg for the Bunny was lost, she became distraught.

> [My daughter] made an egg to leave out for the Easter Bunny. [Then] . . . on 4/14/90 (Holy Saturday) we took the Easter Baskets to be blessed [at my grandmother's old neighborhood church]. My brother has a refrigerator in his basement so it was decided that he would take OUR family's baskets to his house and put them in his extra refrigerator. Well on this evening, when [my daughter] realized the special egg she made for the Easter Bunny was gone, she became QUITE upset. Well, to quiet her down I told her to call [her cousin] and have her write a note to the Easter Bunny and tell him that this egg is for him from [my daughter].

Not only did the cousin write a note to tell the Easter Bunny who the egg was from, but the daughter whose egg had gone astray wrote a note (complete with her aunt's address) to the Easter Bunny explaining the dilemma: "If you come here first the egg is at my aunt's house on the dining room table with the baskets." The offering took on such meaning that mother and daughter were both eager to show me the notes (which they had saved) and to retell the story.

If life indeed traces to an egg, it is also true that a child's vitality becomes associated with the egg through the act of decorative coloring. As Mrs. Hart (a mother, and also a day care provider who colored eggs with her charges) said:

> There's a lot of pride in how they're . . . colored. . . . It's mine. I made that. So it is, there is a certain amount of personal identity attached to those stupid little things.

When giving the egg to the Easter Bunny, the child is making a personal offering in which they have actively invested their own vitality and selfhood. The Easter Bunny, also symbolic of a special sort of vitality (symbolic of nature, early childhood, and even supernatural force), endorses a child's gift by accepting it. In other words, the young ritual participant exerts herself or himself actively in the ritual and in turn is affirmed for doing so.

## A CHILD-ENCOURAGED FESTIVAL

The active involvement of the child is a prominent feature of the cultural activity of Easter, whether it's hunting for or coloring eggs. It is not that the child is actively involved because the parent urges them to do so (as Caplow and Williamson assert in describing Easter as a festival of children's independence);[17] rather, the child urges the parent to implement certain cultural routines. To be sure, tradition plays a part in some family practices. But it is often the child who reminds the parent to color eggs, put up decorations, leave an offering for the Easter Bunny, or even to resume church attendance. This active influence of the child on festival observation directly contradicts expressed views of many social scientists who espouse a more passive view of "socialization." Take, for example, the view of Mary and Herbert Knapp, specialists in children's folklore and peer culture:

> Children have little or nothing to say about how most of the well-known holidays are celebrated. . . . Christmas and Easter are full of folk customs—hanging stockings, decorating the tree, buying new clothes, hunting eggs—but adults define which of these customs will be observed.[18]

My interviews demonstrate that, on the contrary, mothers themselves attribute to children decisive influence on how Easter customs are implemented. In two households, Easter customs would not have been observed at all, had it not been for youngest family members' influential pressure. In one family, the mother and father were not Christian (father was Islamic, mother was Baha'i). But under the pressure of the six-year-old daughter, Mrs. Topp had obtained secular Easter decorations.

> Those cutout pictures in the window, you know, with the bunnies and stuff like that. Which was another thing I'm pressured into doing. Because my daughter's very observant. She'll go around saying, "Oh, they all have their Easter decorations.

They're getting ready for Easter. We better get ready for Easter."

Despite Mr. Topp's hesitancy ("it isn't a religious holiday for him"), Mrs. Topp allowed her daughter and son to color eggs and to have a basket delivery from the Easter Bunny. The daughter had learned about Easter (and "recognized it as the day that Jesus rose from the dead," according to her mother) at her day care center, which was attached to a Baptist church. Her mother felt, on balance, that "these little frivolities" were worth observing so as not to "exclude" her daughter from the experiences of her peers.

In another family, the mother, Mrs. Sark, was a self-described born-again Christian whose like-minded siblings and friends opposed the Easter Bunny custom because of its "roots in paganism." Yet under the influence of her children, Mrs. Sark prepared baskets and let her children color eggs and visit with the Easter Bunny impersonator. She realized that "there are some people that might be a little chagrined to find out that the Easter Bunny . . . comes to my home." Yet "for the kids," who attended public schools and made decorations depicting rabbits and baskets there, she allowed these festival observations to get started. Mrs. Sark even seemed to enjoy these customs herself, although she did not plan to continue them once her children were older.

Even in families where parents willingly made way for the Easter Bunny of their own accord, children influenced the manner in which the festival was celebrated. Mothers tended to downplay the importance of the Easter Bunny, saying, for example, "We really don't make a big deal as far as the Easter Bunny." But children reminded them to color eggs and to prepare for the Bunny's visit. If children experienced a cultural practice at school (e.g., the Easter Bunny came to school, messed up their desks, and left grass all over), this experience could influence practices at home. As one mother said, "I thought it was a neat idea, so I left a few things of grass in the front room." This pattern even extended to church attendance, such as in a family where the daughter, who was enrolled in parochial school, coaxed the mother into attending church ("Now you know you should be takin' me to church").

Overall, parents seem less involved in the mythic structure of the Easter Bunny than in Santa Claus. At Easter, in most families, the adult religious narrative tends to overshadow the children's mythic structure. The Easter Bunny is not felt by adults to be related to the idea of the Resurrection. Conversely, children are even less knowledgeable about the religious narrative associated with Easter than the religious story of Christmas. Children and adults, it seems, observe Easter according to their own, separate mythic practices. But children exert active influence to ensure that the children's cult (Easter eggs, Easter Bunny, baskets, and so on) does not go unobserved. Children's drive to celebrate the festival of Easter in a uniquely childlike way has a discernible impact on family ritual.

# Six

# Commerce, Family, and Meaning:
## *Institutions in Children's Ritual*

St Nicholas Music collects 4.5 cents every time any
recording of "Rudolph the Red Nosed Reindeer" is sold. Radio
time is even better: 18 cents from every station every time it plays the
song. And then there are residuals from the television show,
which has aired over 20 seasons.
—Irena Chalmers, *The Great Christmas Almanac*

Deck the malls with plastic holly.
—Saying from Christmas card

As we have seen, early childhood in contemporary America is associated with anything but materialism. Rather, young children are equated with fantastic thinking and the capacity for mystical, transcendent belief, which Santa Claus, the Easter Bunny, and the Tooth Fairy all encode. Moreover, early childhood is apt to be closely associated with the domain of home and nursery rather than with the domain of commerce (and money) outside the home. (Recall that the money left by the Tooth Fairy is a signal of maturity, not of early childhood.) The institution of the family, whose rituals are so important to the social adjustment and well-being of children, might be said to stand in counterpoint to the rational, adult, money-linked domain of commerce. Yet does it?

Although family ritual both reflects and maintains family values (affirming family bonds, nurturance of offspring, etc.), it does not do so in isolation. Ironically, even while family ritual serves to support the family, an institution at risk, in its traditional form,[1] modern families often rely on commercial institutions outside the family for support to carry out their rituals. Examples of this reliance upon commercial institutions abound in informant interviews and field notes—not to mention, of course, the evidence of the shopping mall impersonators of Santa and the Easter Bunny. From the Easter egg hunt that takes place in the aisles of a grocery store to the charity-sponsored toy collection held at a shopping mall, commercial domains are used for quasi-sacred purposes in children's ritual.

## THE (FAMILY) CHRISTMAS TREE

When families acquire a Christmas tree or a Christmas tree ornament, they generally acquire it through some commercial establishment. Historically, a Christmas tree represented nature brought indoors, the evergreen being an exception to the otherwise bleak winter environment. In modern times, the tree is seldom cut down by the user from its natural woodlands but is likely bought from an urban tree lot. In warm climates, the tree may be trucked far from its natural cold environment and may be tented on a concrete parking lot to protect it from the glaring sun. The tree may even be artificial, brought in not from the outdoors, but down from the attic (or up from the basement) and assembled by human hands.

Scholars studying consumer behavior have noted that some commercially purchased items may hold sacred meaning for the purchaser.[2] No better example of this occurs to me than the Christmas tree, which is by no means a profane product to its owners, despite its commercial source.

Among both adults and children, the decorated Christmas tree serves as a dominant symbol, in Victor Turner's sense of the phrase. A dominant symbol contains a condensation of multiple meanings, encapsulating the major properties of the ritual process. Among the properties of ritual is its role to "convert the obligatory into the desirable," to shed positive light on socially sanctioned activity.[3] The Christmas tree thus symbolizes and reinforces family bonds and the family nurturing of children, social norms made to seem desirable at Christmas.

One aspect of the Christmas tree's meanings involves its preordained role as a place to "pile the presents." Family-exchanged gifts and gifts from Santa Claus are located under the tree. In effect, the Christmas tree serves as a kind of beacon or guide for placing the gifts. (Christmas gifts, of course, are themselves affirming of family ties, especially the loving nurturance of parents for children.)[4] Children explained how important the Christmas tree is from this perspective.

[Girl, six:] You put up a tree in your house, so he [Santa] can put presents under it.

[Boy, six:] He [Santa] can slide down the chimney and continue to lead somewhere inside your house, . . . finds your Christmas tree and puts a lot of presents under it.

[Girl, seven:] [If someone forgot to put up a tree], wherever they put the Christmas tree, he [Santa] would probably put the presents there.

Santa Claus (in the guise of his shopping mall impersonator) was observed to ask *half* the children who visited him whether their Christmas tree was "up yet." Santa's question implied that the ritual would not come to pass properly unless the Christmas tree was up and decorated, that the family must be "ready for Christmas." Santa gave each child who visited him a cardboard Christmas tree and stick-on ornaments to decorate it, further symbolic evidence that Santa considered Christmas trees important. In a typical exchange between Santa and a child (who in this case was a three-year-old boy), Santa praised the decorated tree.

SANTA: Are you getting ready for Christmas? Do you have your Christmas tree up yet?
CHILD: Yeah.
SANTA: You have! Oh!
CHILD: It has ornaments on it.
SANTA: Oh, that's good.

In the fullest sense of the phrase, the Christmas tree is a family tree. The ornaments decorating the tree are repositories of deep, family-related meaning—having been collected gradually over the years of family formation and growth. In many cases, ornaments were hand made by the children in the family and displayed with pride and care. In other instances, children were given a gift of an ornament each year, with the plan that they will take with them their own ornaments upon growing up and forming a separate family unit. Not infrequently, ornaments were personalized with the child's name. Occasionally, children's photographs were part of the ornament. Iconography associated with early childhood was a common subject matter for ornaments: Mickey Mouse and other Disney characters, teddy bears, clowns, rocking horses, toy soldiers, Sesame Street characters, and so on. (A toy train set up on the floor to run the perimeter of the Christmas tree captures a similar child-oriented theme.) In one way or another, children adorn the Christmas tree through the idiom of the ornaments—making it a family tree.

Because the ornaments decorating a tree are not all acquired at once and reflect a cumulative history, the tree conveys a discernible perception of family continuity and temporal connectedness. Informants' own words capture this sense of continuity and meaningfulness among mothers.

Every ornament we have has some kind of personal significance, where somebody in the family could say, "I bought that here, I bought that there." Like sometimes we'll be on vacation and we'll get an ornament. . . . It's kind of a summation of family experience, too. Just because the things that we decorate it with, it brings back a lot of family memories. . . . I can remember, like, those little blue booties, someone gave those to me when I was expecting [my daughter]. . . . And then across there, there's a 6, a yellow 6. Well, she got that on her sixth birthday. . . . I guess I would say it's kind of a summation of different family experiences, and for that reason it's more special, too.

All those ornaments that we have, when we got married we didn't just go out and buy a couple boxes of ornaments and stick them on the tree. All the ornaments that we have are ornaments that we've gotten since the first year we got married.

. . . Every year, we've gotten, like, Hallmark ornaments with dates on them, or all of [my daughter's] ornaments she made in school. . . . so all those ornaments, maybe somebody gave it to us for some special reason or something. They're not just a box of ornaments we bought and stuck them on the tree. They're special ornaments. . . . I suppose [they represent] a part of our life over the years since we got married, and since we got [my daughter] and the boys. You know, they have their "baby's first Christmas" ornaments on there.

We've got them, like the "first baby" ones. And I've got some that were like from when I was a little girl, and my mom just kind of outgrew them, and then we took our share. . . . We've got one from a [pet] bird that we had, that's from 1979 when we bought our bird. I mean, the bird's been gone for a while, but that still goes up there 'cause that's our bird's ornament. And just the ones they [the children] made at school, which there's probably about thirty of them. We save them and put them up. . . . [The ornaments represent] all the years that you've been together. Memories of when they were little. And we've got stuff that they've made at school stuck all over the house.

[The tree represents] memories, memories. We have ornaments that my husband and I made the first year we were married. . . . The kids made some last year. . . . Or people gave us some. I don't go out and buy balls or ornaments in boxes. . . . We have ones from when they [the children] were born, you know, their first Christmas ornaments. . . . We have ornaments that have stuff to do with fishing, because my husband loves fishing. We have ornaments that have to do with . . . when they were babies. We have ornaments that have to do with pictures of the kids when they've been different stages. . . . [My feeling about it is] it's just Christmas . . . kind of an emotional thing. [Eyes fill with tears:] Family. Family. Love.

From memorializing a deceased pet to recalling a child's birth and first Christmas, Christmas tree ornaments ultimately are not

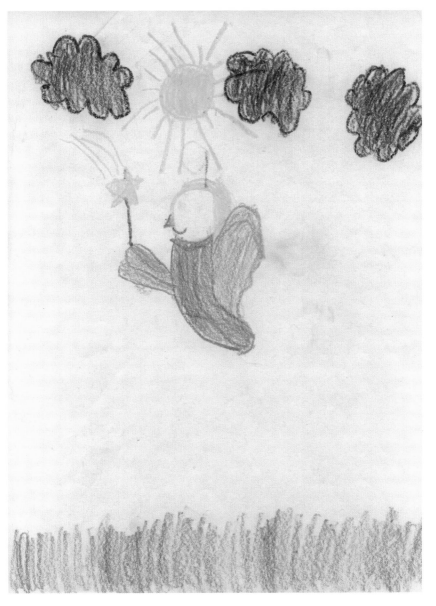

The Tooth Fairy imagined by a seven-year-old girl was angellike—with wings, halo, and a magic wand—flying close to the clouds.

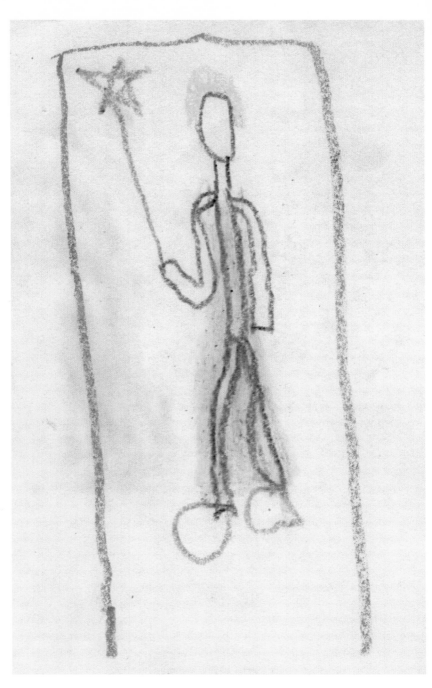

The Tooth Fairy's intervention involves an almost spiritlike or liminal presence; a six-year-old boy drew the fairy in translucent dress hovering at the threshold of a room.

Pastel colors were often used in depicting the Tooth Fairy: the drawing by a seven-year-old boy shows a tiny specterlike fairy, yet ironically with currency in hand.

A seven-year-old girl provided a typical portrait of Santa: with aged appearance (grey hair and beard) and an outline of the conspicuous red clothing that allows people to "see him better."

In this drawing by a six-year-old boy, the triangle shape of the house Santa visits echoes that of the Christmas tree (with presents beneath). Santa flies above the wintry scene, as Rudolph leads the way.

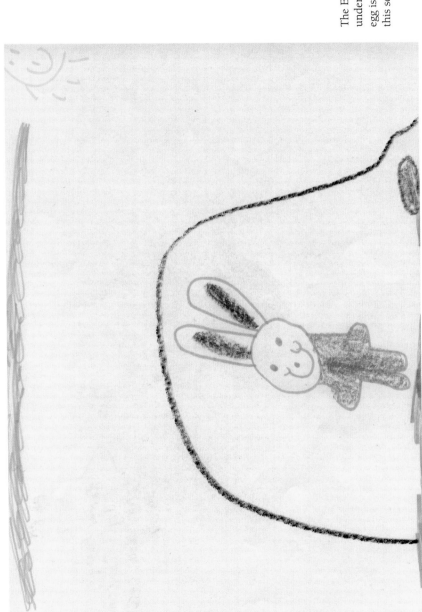

The Easter Bunny lives in an underground warren (where an egg is also kept), according to this seven-year-old girl.

Children envisioned the Easter Bunny as more animallike than personified. The lack of clothes on this typically white bunny (drawn by a seven-year-old girl) and the active feeling of "hopping very fast" differ markedly from many adult-drawn, commercial depictions.

The Easter Bunny is a spiritual, transcendent figure as the barely seen bunny in this picture by a seven-year-old girl illustrates.

so much ornamental as expressive. Taken together, they serve to integrate into a holistic symbol—the Christmas tree—a family's history and ongoing union.

Mihaly Csikszentmihalyi and Eugene Rochberg-Halton describe a family for whom their Christmas tree ornaments were a treasured possession. Consistent with current findings, the wife in this family called the ornaments a "review of my married life."[5] As if to highlight the implicit meaning of family communion and continuity, the father was writing out a kinship record (another sort of "family tree"), although he did not consciously relate his kinship research to the physical tree decorated in ornaments.

Scholars studying family ritual have pointed out that this kind of symbolic activity can aid family members in making transitions within the family life cycle, such as the changes that occur with initial family formation.[6] Symbolic ritual can be an abbreviated metaphor for the warmth, comfort, relatedness, and support of the family.[7] It can also help to accommodate change by welcoming new members ("baby's first Christmas" ornaments), bidding good-bye to those leaving the nest (by presenting them with their share of ornaments), announcing loss (symbolizing deceased members), and countless other transmissions of meaning.

When two people marry, each brings to the marriage a separate ritual system from their family of origin, out of which a new family ritual emerges that involves abandoning some parts of the past. In effect, the separate ritual systems of husband and wife are filtered through, and a joint ritual is selectively forged that maximizes the felt significance for the entire family. Thus, family formation plays itself out symbolically through family ritual, a process verified by these informants.

In one family, for instance, a new ritual evolved, using a "real" Christmas tree, as had been the custom within the husband's family of origin, but retaining, by means of ritualized joking, a memory of the wife's artificial tree from childhood. Continuity with the childhood family rituals of both spouses was thus maintained.

When I was small we used to have an aluminum tree. And I thought, it didn't even faze me in the least why we had an aluminum tree. Then when I met my husband, he goes, "Oh, you have an aluminum tree." And ever since we got married he had to have a real tree. And this year, now I'm used to it. And now he kidded me, and he said, "Well, maybe we should get a fake tree." And I said, "No, no, no." I said, "You have to have a real tree." I said, "It just seems better having a real tree."

Just as family unity finds a metaphor in the Christmas tree, so too does the tree provide a metaphor for family tensions and emotions. Feelings such as irritation, sorrow, excitement, and joy are cathected upon the tree itself. Consider, for example, fighting over what species of evergreen to buy, or fighting over who gets to hang certain ornaments on the tree. Or consider a family that experienced the death of the paternal grandmother shortly before Christmas and hesitated to set up their Christmas tree at all.

> I wasn't even going to put up the Christmas tree. My mother-in-law just passed away, and we were not really celebrating a lot. So that's why we took [the tree] down early.

Another informant, who had inherited an artificial Christmas tree upon the death of her husband's mother, had videotaped relatives standing next to the tree. (The practice of photographing family members "under the tree" is common—another tree-family connection.) In the years since her videotaping, some of these relatives had died. The Christmas tree served to modulate, one senses, her feelings of loss.

> My husband's mother died before we got married . . . and since that time, my father has died, and his brother, and my godfather, and several, like my grandmother, his grandmother, and each year in our videotape, we have the tree and one of those people by it. So it's nice. That's what the tree reminds me of. And one year it almost fell on my dad. So I have a lot of memories of the tree.

Gananath Obeyesekere has called attention to "the capacity of the symbolic idiom to operate simultaneously at different levels—intrapsychic, interpersonal or sociological, and cultural."[8] As individuals drawn from a pluralistic, commerce-oriented society interact to form and maintain a common family culture, they obtain meaning on both an individual and a shared level. Precisely because the symbolic structure is simultaneously personal and social, shared meaning can be maintained. The Christmas tree is both a personal symbol of family life and a shared family symbol. It is purchased from the commercial sector (as perhaps, are its Hallmark ornaments), but its meaning is provided by the owner. American Christmas ritual reveals how ritual symbolism—while reflecting a constraining force of past tradition—ultimately relies upon the ongoing dynamic of meaningfulness to individuals for its sustenance. Children, as well as adults, contribute to the way meaning is sustained within family ritual.

## NATIVITY AND THE (FAMILY) TREE

In an insightful comparison of the Christmas tree and the traditional Nativity scene (featuring the baby Jesus, parents Mary and Joseph, and a few farm animals), Shirley Park Lowry has pointed out that both the Nativity scene and the Christmas tree are typically represented with a star at the top.[9] Pictorial illustrations work better than words to illustrate her comparison.

Observe further that an angel is sometimes substituted for the star, either above the tree or above the Nativity scene. Both angel and star signify cosmic, protective forces that call attention to and "watch over" the family scene or, in the case of the Christmas

tree, the family tree. Thus the Christmas idiom depicts the nuclear family as under cosmic attention and protection.

Parents who train their children in the religious meaning of Christmas, a common activity, emphasize the Nativity as a narrative for children to learn. (By contrast, the Resurrection narrative is less commonly learned by children.) Christmas pageants, in which children dress up and reenact the Nativity story, are common at Sunday school and parochial school. Thus, opportunities for children to absorb the full iconography of the Nativity—not only Jesus, Mary, and Joseph, but also the shepherds and the Magi—abound. Yet in interviews, children typically limited their discussion to the nuclear family when describing the characters in the decorative crèche present in many households: Jesus and his parents were readily identified, but the shepherds and the Magi were far less salient to six- and seven-year-old children. Note an exemplary case in which Charlie (age six) revealed his awareness of the importance of the nuclear family for raising babies, such as Jesus:

> CDC: In front of your house, there's a picture [decoration] of something.
> CHARLIE: Yeah, with Jesus in there and Joseph and Mary.
> CDC: Baby Jesus in there, and Joseph and Mary. Who are they?
> CHARLIE: Jesus' parents.
> CDC: Why are they out there?
> CHARLIE: Because Jesus was a baby at that time. He couldn't take care of hisself.

Time and again, children described Christmas as Jesus' birthday—birthdays being an occasion for family ritual (including gifts) in which a child's birth is celebrated. (Several families prepared a birthday cake with candles as part of their Christmas celebration, to remind children that the real purpose of Christmas is to celebrate Jesus' birth.) Birthday rituals are highly salient to children, who can easily describe the procedure by which candles are put on a cake, illuminated (not unlike Christmas lights), and blown out while making a wish (heard by God, as one girl explained it), after a song is sung for the benefit of the "birthday child" (analogous to Christmas carols). The Nativity celebrated at

Christmas is easily framed from a child's perspective as a surrogate birthday party. In this way, the presents received by contemporary children are proxy gifts, necessarily given to a living child, since "Jesus is in heaven," where "there are no birthday cakes" or presents.

So construed, Christmas becomes a holiday that celebrates the birth of a Child—and through the Nativity, also celebrates the role of the nuclear family, signified by Mary and Joseph, in caring for that helpless, dependent infant.

If parents complain (only half-jokingly) about the expense of purchasing Christmas gifts ("If there was no more Santa Claus, it would save me a lot of money"), they are in effect making a commentary on the burden of raising a family—a burden given sacred status and purpose through the trope of the Nativity. Like the Christmas tree, with its ornaments commemorating the birth or first Christmas of a family's own children, the Nativity scene symbolizes the nuclear family and its role in raising a dependent child. Since at Christmas children receive proxy gifts from an extraordinary visitor, Santa Claus, a symbolic equation is set up between the miracle of the Christ child's birth and the specialness of each and every child. The birth of a child, in and of itself, is taken to be a miraculous event worthy of an astounding presentation of gifts.

The dependence of children upon parents, albeit the expected order of things in contemporary America, is a relationship so unbalanced as to be striking. As Caplow writes:

> Parents . . . are supposed to devote a large part of their total resources to educating, caring for, and entertaining their children. The reciprocal duties of children towards parents are light. They are not expected or required to make any material contribution to their parents at any time within their lives, and they are not answerable to law or public opinion if they show no permanent attachments to them.[10]

Of course, children's "delight" (upon Santa's visitation) makes an immaterial return to parents, who enjoy childlike wonder and excitement, albeit vicariously. The cult of the Nativity and the cult of Santa Claus both serve to provide a focus of attention for adults that reinforces their responsibilities toward children. And both cults pronounce children to be creatures of wonder, worthy of unreciprocated caring and associated with awe.

## YULETIDE COMMERCIALISM: MATERIAL TREASURES

Just as a commercially purchased Christmas tree can have personal, felt meaning that is as sanctified, in many ways, as a Nativity scene, other artifacts from the commercial domain can also be symbolically important to ritual participants. The shopping mall Santa, the commercially conceived Rudolph the Red-Nosed Reindeer, characters from Disney, and the Sears wish book all figure into the treasured experience of family Christmas ritual. Even specific department stores (in Chicago, the downtown store of Marshall Field's) can have special meaning to families, taking on an importance that might be regarded as sacred. Often, suburbanites who otherwise never ventured downtown annually drove their children into town to see the decorated windows at Marshall Field's, to have lunch under the Field's Christmas tree, and to visit Santa there. (Parents maintained, at times, that the Field's Santa Claus was the only "real," authentic one.) On the Friday after Thanksgiving, seventy-five thousand shoppers descend on Marshall Field's (versus the usual twenty to twenty-five thousand), showing that the custom of visiting Field's at Christmas is widespread indeed.[11]

Purchased Christmas lights (garishly adorning the household exterior) also are a material good from which special sustenance and meaning is derived by festival participants. As a seasonal rite of passage marking the darkest time of the year, Christmas occurs at a time in need of excitement, as well as light. The winter solstice provides a natural symbol of bleakness and containment against which man-made decorations can light up the cold and darkness.

Far from profane, the material goods purchased at Christmas are apt to be steeped in special meaning. Nevertheless, the native charge that "Christmas has become too commercialized" was recited like a mantra by adult participants in the festival of Christmas. Time and again, complaints were heard that merchants "rush the season" by promoting Christmas merchandise too far in advance. As for the bounty of gifts from Santa Claus, some adults worried that Santa's gifts, too, risk the teaching of materialism and greed. Mothers continually claimed that they didn't think it was good for children to "get everything they ask for"—since material desires were needful of limitation.

One scholar of consumer behavior, Russell Belk, has similarly criticized Santa Claus for teaching materialistic values:

> If Santa is god, he is the god of materialism. His bag is a cornucopia and the stockings he fills are miniature replicas of this cornucopia. Both Santa and attendant seasonal rituals (these include huge family feasts, office parties, New Year's Eve parties, and even the large circulation of Christmas issues of *Playboy* magazine) celebrate greed, gluttony, and hedonism. The one-way gifts from a munificent Santa to children encourage the views that the world is full of good things and that if one simply deserves it, material wishes will come true. Thus American society has reflected its deepest values onto Santa Claus.[12]

Yet coming to terms with Christmas commercialism requires embracing a paradox. Stated simply, the material way in which children are showered with gifts at Christmas is the very behavior responsible for putting materialism on trial, at Christmas. The abundance of material consumption apparent at Christmastime paradoxically serves to evoke criticism about all this consumption. (By some estimates, Christmas gift-giving constitutes a $37 billion market in America.)[13]

This kind of parody through exaggeration is typical of festival ambience. Anthropologists have endorsed the notion that the multiplication of such symbolic content as fireworks, masks, or fantastic clothing within a festival (until such content is nonsensically parodied) serves to suspend customary social meanings.[14] The paradox of the exaggerated materialism of Christmas is that it causes adults to be critical of materialism—to validate values of family ties, childhood, and nonmaterial wonder, rather than the physical gifts that give symbolic expression to nonmaterial values. Ultimately, Santa's overabundant gifts have a very nonmaterial meaning to adults.

Children, too, are not totally Scrooge-like in their take on Christmas. They learn more than greed from Christmas. In the same spirit as the folk belief that receiving love as a child enables one to give love as an adult, children are said to learn generosity from Christmas, over time. When young informants talked about their experiences with buying gifts for family, or participating in drives to provide for needy families at Christmas, they clearly enjoyed such acts of giving.

Observing Christmas practices in one of America's most apparently commercial locations—the shopping mall—I found that the paradoxical meaning of commerce at Christmas was undeniable. Not only was the Santa Claus impersonator in the mall where I observed given free rein to give free gifts to children, regardless of whether a photo of the child with Santa was purchased by the family, but other acts of generosity also took place in a seemingly natural way in the unexpected domain of the shopping mall. Free entertainment (carolers and musicians), free treats (cookies, cocoa, and cider), and even free horse-and-carriage rides (an old-fashioned image when set against modern, automobile-crowded streets) were provided at various shopping centers.

At one "grand opening" celebration of the arrival of Santa Claus at a mall, a marine band was playing "Santa Claus Is Coming to Town," and kids were walking around carrying red and green balloons. The band was promoting the marines' Toys for Tots program with a poster to that effect and a barrel to collect toys for their charitable distribution. In a commercial setting of a mall, charitable generosity was being touted (by the marines). Walking past the band, I noticed a young man and young woman laying out cookies and milk on a long table, to be given out free of charge, courtesy of the mall. A little child of four or so gave their balloon, also handed out by the mall, to the lady who was giving out cookies, a show of generosity at which the woman smiled warmly. She, in turn, gave the child her paper hat, which looked like a Santa cap. An exchange of generosities.

In the apparently commercial setting of a shopping mall, then, a child can receive a lesson in generosity by "playing Santa" and giving away a balloon (receiving, appropriately, a Santa hat for this act) or by participating in a charitable toy donation drive.[15] This grand opening celebration, which also included a famous TV clown for children to visit with and receive an autographed picture from, as well as costumed characters depicting a trick-performing elf, a reindeer, and a polar bear, created a distinctive impression. The aura at the mall was festive and child oriented. Few people were carrying bags as if they'd done much shopping. Generosity seemed just as pervasive as commercialism.

Ira Zepp, a professor of religious studies, has argued that the contemporary American shopping mall has religious dimensions as a "ceremonial center."[16] Designed as a "centered space" resembling cathedrals in some respects, a mall is a center for festival celebration and community gathering, as a substitute for "ancient sacred centers." Whether or not Zepp's view is correct in its particulars, he nevertheless has insight into the paradoxical, non-commercial uses to which a shopping mall can be put. The expressive content of a culture, which, in contemporary American society, is largely encoded through commercialized structures, can seldom be read through a straight lens. Paradoxical, sacred meaning lies beneath apparently commercial, materialistic entities: from mass-produced lights and plastic Christmas trees to department stores and malls.

## EASTER COMMERCIALISM: COMMERCE MEETS NATURE

Like Christmas, the Easter festival is dependent on commercial institutions for its ritual. This holds true even though nature is the referent behind much of the content of the festival. Not only is there the Easter Bunny impersonator, but also purchased candy, manufactured grass, and new clothes worn on Easter Sunday.

Mothers had little praise for the delivery of candy to children via the Easter Bunny. The lack of nutritional legitimacy associated with candy had led a few mothers to cut down on the amount given, or (in one instance) to "hide some of it in the freezer," or to give sugarless candy. Nevertheless, candy was still the mainstay of the Easter Bunny's bounty. Candy, mothers felt, provided an oral, primitive enjoyment that children would miss if they substituted something else. (Thus, children's expected reactions have a discernible influence on basket-giving practices.) Some of the traditional candies contributed symbolic meaning as well, such as "marshmallow peeps" (confectionery chicks emblematic of baby animals) or jelly beans (a bean is of course egg shaped, as well as something that grows).

Intriguingly, several Chicago adults felt that the only Easter candy that would be "right" (that is, conform to the expected traditions from their own childhood) was made by Fannie May, the Chicago candy merchants. "Ever since I was a little kid I got something with Fannie May," one such mother explained to me, gesturing for me to try some of the Fannie May brand candy her own children had received. Clearly, a sense of connectedness with the past can derive from buying a particular brand of Easter candy (or from visiting the right department store at Christmas, as when visiting Santa at Marshall Field's). Not just heirlooms, but an item as perishable as a chocolate rabbit, provided it is from Fannie May, can provide a sense of completeness and continuity.

Along with the candy in the Easter basket, mothers placed commercially sold, imitation grass. This green, shredded cellophane-like substance was almost always present (only two mothers had eliminated the grass, substituting tissue paper). Yet mothers had very little praise for the grass, which they felt to be "messy" and problematic. Time and again, a facial expression connoting disgust would descend upon a mother's face as she described how this artificial grass "gets everywhere." Like nature itself, which the grass clearly signifies (being "springy," "green," "growing," and from "outdoors"), the grass was apt to get out of control and to permeate the household. The "wretched cellulose" required endless vacuuming—much like the fallen needles from a live Christmas tree. Yet because "the children expect it to be there," and out of a sense of tradition, this messiness was generally tolerated as a part of the Easter festival celebration.

In *Purity and Danger*, Mary Douglas reminds us that while

disorder spoils pattern, it also provides the materials of a less restrictive, more potent pattern.[17] The potent force implicitly signified by the celluloid grass in the Easter basket is natural grass— and thereby the life-giving properties of nature. As Mrs. Gloor said,

> [Grass] makes me feel good. Growth, sunshine . . . It makes you feel good just to think that the grass is there. And not only that, you see it grow. It makes you think about God. . . . It makes you see life itself. Grass.

When children, also symbolic of growth and life, play with the grass from their Easter basket and "get it all over the house," the household becomes permeated with life. New life is metaphorically spread throughout the house (children, again, being instrumental in this) in celluloid representation. Mothers dislike this pollutant, grass being welcome in a suburban lawn, not inside. But like confetti at New Year's or rice at a wedding, the grass that is strewn at Easter encodes the vitality of a new beginning: spring and, perhaps, the Resurrection.

Also significant of a new beginning are the new clothes often purchased for children for the Easter celebration. The practice many times was recalled from mothers' own childhoods. New clothes are symbolic of renewal in general, a way of "cleaning up your act" or "getting a fresh start." (Spring cleaning of the house encodes a similar meaning.) Children themselves seldom mentioned getting new clothing as a part of Easter, but to mothers it was a salient practice. Since warmer weather was imminent, and since children had grown in the past winter, buying new clothes was a practical response to the processes of nature, as well as an expressive act.

Even in an industrial society, Easter is, in part, a seasonal rite of passage. Awareness that nature renews itself and that young animals (of which the Easter Bunny is aptly representative) are born in spring is not lost on urbanite adults. Commercially purchased products can help a person to achieve oneness with the natural world, to "join with mother nature," as one mother put it. As Mrs. Iris expressed it:

It's always been new beginnings, you know, new clothes. . . .
It helps you get away with the winter doldrums for one thing.
It helps you get back in the groove from all the New Year's
resolutions you didn't keep. I think it's just human nature to
join with mother nature. And all the new beginnings we notice,
the flowers coming up and the grass sprouting and the trees
sprouting and the little lamb. People want to join that too, you
know. They want to—perhaps you feel closer to God, I guess.
Closer to earth. Closer to mother nature.

## EATING AND GATHERING

Gathering together for a meal with the extended family is a form
of celebration common to both Easter and Christmas. An ideal
type behind this collective meal can be seen in a widely repro-
duced painting by the American artist Norman Rockwell, depicting a family gathered at a dining room table, as the white-
haired grandmother carries in the turkey to the rapt attention of
all. The point encoded by the Rockwell painting is the collectivity
of the meal: The family eats a single turkey (prepared by a woman,
but carved by the male household head) as an icon of their togetherness. To mothers, this collective meal is the culmination of the
holiday gathering. Still, the food need not be turkey. At Christmas, the food eaten can be ham, lasagna, seafood, pizza, or ethnic
foods gathered from the tradition of a particular family. Easter
dinner could be lamb, ham, or turkey. Note that pizza, ham,
lasagna, or lamb can convey a message comparable to the one
conveyed by turkey: that the act of eating unifies the family, since
the family eats from a jointly shared dish.

Included in this unity are not only members of the nuclear
family, but typically the extended family as well: cousins, aunts,
uncles, grandparents. Activities at the Christmas meal might include singing, exchanging gifts, reminiscing about earlier times
together, card playing, or general conversation (among adults).
Whether at Easter or Christmas, the dinner was felt by informants
to bring "togetherness," to strengthen family ties in an era when
social trends such as geographic mobility keep the family apart.

Unity can be so important to such gatherings that when a

family experiences divisions, for instance divorce, parties to a divorce may not participate in these celebrations. Such exclusion is not always planned; sometimes it just "happens": Members might gather with the wife's side of the family, but not the husband's side—if that side of the family has experienced numerous divorces. As one mother said, "I have another brother who's just going through a divorce. So we didn't really see him. I don't know why, but we didn't see him." Family gatherings at Christmas and Easter are consciously symbolic of family cohesion.

Sally Moore and Barbara Myerhoff have pointed out that since ritual is a good form for conveying a message as if it were unquestionable, it is often used to convey those very messages that are most dubitable.[18] Holiday dinner shores up shared family experience. When individuals locate themselves within a symbolic order that transcends the individual, family is a key institution of reference. Yet contemporary adults fear for the prognosis of family life. At Easter and Christmas alike, gathering the family together for a shared meal has become an important priority for adult women. Often, this was the first, the most salient event of Christmas mentioned in interviews with adults. Family ties provide a stability and a sense of tradition in a changing world, where constantly recurring "renewal," much of it not allied with seasonal change, needs to be balanced by continuity.

## MATERIAL MEANS, IMMATERIAL ENDS

It has been stated elsewhere that consumers create transcendent meaning in their lives by sacralizing objects consumed.[19] Ritual is one means by which such sacralization occurs, an observation solidly confirmed by this study. Ritual devices used for holiday symbolism (e.g., the Christmas tree, celluloid Easter grass) can take on strongly felt meaning. The intensity of this meaning all but denies the manufactured origin of ersatz natural objects. A particular brand of Easter chocolate or department store Santa or a particular dish served for holiday dinner can take on meaningful authenticity. The meaning system has such power that even greed can be rendered rejectable by none other than commercial goods, as the proliferation of gifts at Christmas parodies materialism itself.

Marketers sometimes refer to brand-name products with sacralized meaning as possessing a "halo effect." When informants' personal experience is taken seriously, this angelic term takes on an apt tone and needn't be treated with cynicism. No matter how worldly the entity or good, transcendent qualities can be abstracted to a remarkable degree—perhaps especially so at Christmas and Easter.

# Seven

# Flights of Fancy, Leaps of Faith:
## *Issues of Consequence*

In a secular age, children have become the last
sacred objects.
—Joseph Epstein

Children are entitled to their otherness, as anyone else is.
—Alastair Reid

I have a place where dreams are born
And time is never planned
It's not on any chart
You must find it with your heart
Never, never land.
—Song from *Peter Pan,* stage
version

This book deals with the visitation of such immaterial beings as Santa Claus, the Easter Bunny, and the Tooth Fairy. Yet the experiences reported are by no means immaterial in the sense of lacking import or consequence. Santa Claus, the Easter Bunny, and the Tooth Fairy are significant, first of all, for understanding children's active participation in culture. By talking to and observing children, one sees that young cultural members are influential contributors to the dynamics of these rituals. Youngsters are not just passively socialized by adults. Particularly for Easter, children shape cultural practices in an active manner. The young occupy positions of cultural power during ritual practices and are not just receptively acculturated by them.

Second, the engagement of children with the childhood pantheon (the Bunny, the Fairy, and Santa) reveals a psychological experience that is dynamic and complex. Mythological experience, including religious experience, seems to be made possible by a special capacity to cognitively suspend disbelief while engaging one's trust and creative involvement. The individual believer, when given creative leeway respected by others, keeps a mythological figure "alive" partly by sheer force of imaginal playfulness and acceptance. Appreciation for the special, even paradoxical, nature of the mental and emotional capacity for faith is crucial. To treat imaginal experience otherwise—as a circumstance in which children misjudge fantasy for reality, for instance—misses the lesson that childlike faith can best teach.

Since both of these issues, the active role of children in cultural practices and the nature of imaginal experience, are substantial indeed, I will give both some serious attention in this final chapter.

## CHILDREN AS ACTIVE CULTURAL CONTRIBUTORS

In her autobiography, Margaret Mead, a seminal investigator of children's culture, writes of taking her own grandchild to visit Santa Claus.

> Not long before Christmas a television program showed a group of miserable children who were screaming and fearful of the department store Santa Claus onto whose lap they were reluctantly pulled. For any child who saw this televised scene, it was a prescription for fear and dread. However, Catherine and I took Vanni [my granddaughter] downtown to see Santa Claus. On the lower floors of the department store she rollicked through the aisles, got lost under stacks of bargain dresses, and emerged laughing to mock any effort to dampen her delight. Upstairs, we stood in the long, roped-off line of waiting parents and children, the children becoming more anxious by the minute as they were constrained by their parents to stand still, while Vanni raced up and down the line swinging the ropes that bound us in. As they approached Santa many of the children squirmed and fretted and some of them

screamed, as they had been instructed by television to do. But Vanni, sitting contentedly on Santa's lap, "niced" his beard . . . as she had learned to do by stroking the fur of cats, the coats of dogs, and the smooth hair of other children.[1]

Mead's depiction of her granddaughter's Santa Claus visit reflects the views of childhood socialization prevailing during the era of her work. Applying a social learning model, she assumes that children learn "fear and dread," being "instructed by television." Thus, socialization implies a unidirectional process by which children take in the adult-given culture.

But this current study reveals that children's role in cultural practices is not unidirectional. Children influence the interactive process of culture in two ways. First, the symbolic association of children with certain cultural values (including nature, as well as the capacity for wonder and awe) gives them implicit influence within ritual practices. Second, children directly affect cultural practices through their own actions: Children initiate festival observations within their family (such as coloring Easter eggs) and at times serve to modify or preserve the content of existing practices.

A pervasive instance of the symbolic influence of children involves imaginal activity. So fundamental is the association of young children with imaginal experience that members of our culture view the capacity for fantasy and imaginal experience as inextricably linked (in a reverse direction) to developmental growth. Imaginal activity, in other words, is something a child should "grow out of." Children who make contact with an "imaginary companion" are thought to be normal: engaging in behavior that is "intrinsically appealing,"[2] environment-enriching,[3] and contributing a "positive role" to their lives.[4] Yet according to social norms, children are to abandon this imaginal activity as they get older; when an adult makes contact with an imaginal rabbit, mental illness is imputed (as dramatized in the play *Harvey*)—at least ordinarily.[5]

Perhaps because American adults have little license to engage in imaginal activity (outside the confines of religious orthodoxy, literature and the other arts, dreams, and private speech and thought), they rely on vicarious experience, via their children, to reenter the "wonder years" of the developmental past. Mothers find perceptible enrichment by doing this, and Christmas (like a Disneyland pilgrimage or a visit by the Tooth Fairy) provides an ideal occasion for such enrichment. Santa Claus represents a "cargo cult" of idealized gifts for children—and in turn provides an experience (at root, vicarious) of wonder and repose for adults.[6] An excerpt from my interview with Mrs. Taylor illustrates this sentiment.

> They're just so excited, and everything to them is magical. . . . There's just something about Christmas, the excitement, and that they, it's like they come alive. . . . They don't see the world as it really is [laughter]. They're naive. I think to them, magic and that, oh, I think they stay up on the high because they don't have to get to the reality of work, and you know, normal living.

It should not go unemphasized, however, that relying on children's belief as a source of adult vicarious experience gives children a powerful role within the ritual as a whole. If children are cynical about Santa, or unmoved by Santa's magical gift delivery,[7] adults will be let down in their attempts to idealize Christmas (since adults identify with children). Children's responses to adults' actions at Christmas (their choice of gifts, the leaving of an offering for Santa, etc.) are instrumental to the success of the ritual. When children do not respond as adults would like, modifications follow. Consider an example from the literature on family ritual. The informant is fifty-one.

> I would try in the beginning when the children were small to read the message from the Gospel, from St. Luke, and The Night Before Christmas. They weren't really interested, though. Somehow it didn't come across. We've started a new tradition now. At least one thing that you give has to be homemade. We started that just a few years ago.[8]

At Christmas, then, children's perceptions and reactions have an impact on family ritual and even on the myth of Santa Claus. For example, children have mythologized Rudolph the Red-nosed Reindeer, who guides Santa's sleigh with his bright red nose, an element of the Santa Claus myth often overlooked by adults. To leave out Rudolph seems mistaken to most children, who have embraced this misfit hero as so real that they often leave Rudolph an offering of carrot or apple on Christmas Eve. (Rudolph conforms to a motif common in children's folklore—the "ugly duckling" motif; in that motif, the very trait that makes someone a misfit is found to yield outstanding talent or specialness.) Rudolph was left out of the story in the movie *Ernest Saves Christmas,* a fact about which juvenile moviegoers (in the audience I observed) complained aloud. When recalling how they once looked up into the sky and saw Santa's sleigh, informants sometimes said they saw Rudolph also.

Children's faith in the Tooth Fairy is an issue taken seriously by American mothers, who prefer to guard their children's belief and to keep them youthfully dependent ("under my wings"). Such intentions notwithstanding, children interpret the Tooth Fairy's gift as one that bestows maturity and power. The Tooth Fairy ritual is more interactive and more empowering of the child than even mothers suspect, since children interpret the Tooth Fairy's transaction through a different lens (with a more "mature" focus) than do mothers. Children feel older as a result of losing their baby teeth and getting money. Blind to this perception, mothers believe that the ritual, because of the "magical" Fairy, keeps children young.

At Easter, children are associated not only with imaginal thought, but also with nature and growth, key referential values for that festival. It is tempting to hypothesize that American children themselves embrace Easter customs with active intensity (coloring and hunting for eggs, especially) largely because they themselves identify with life and growth. Perhaps children are natural symbols of nature asserting itself with all its uncontrollability and are thereby consonant in association (even self-association) with Easter. Regardless, children do independently, actively shape the cultural practices at Easter by initiating family rituals and by shaping (or resisting undesired change to) those rituals.

Children have autonomous impact, then, on what they believe and how they implement a ritual. This suggests that in order to understand the process of culture where children are involved, the child's active voice in the cultural process had best be heard and taken into account. While this has been recognized with regard to the study of children's autonomous peer culture,[9] conventional models have often assumed that a unidirectional socialization operates in adult-child cultural practices.

To understand culture in its full complexity, it is important to assess both juvenile and adult viewpoints and dynamically interrelate them. When a child interacts with an adult in a jointly constructed cultural event, the child's point of view may not accord with the adult's perspective, contrary to Mead's supposition.[10] Taking children into account more than enriches ethnographic understanding; it enables understanding of the full social dynamic in the first place.[11]

Suzanne Gaskins and John Lucy apply a similar argument to the Yucatec Maya:

> Although children form a significant segment of the population in most societies, descriptions of their activities comprise a relatively insignificant fraction of most ethnographic accounts. . . . Even ethnographies devoted entirely to descriptions of children and their development generally conform to this pattern: child life is described in terms of its trajectory towards adult forms and children are not credited with any significant or distinctive role in the production of social organization or culture. In our fieldwork among the Yucatec Maya, we have found that Yucatec children have a substantial and distinctive impact on the structuring and operation of the culture as a whole. . . . Certain aspects of Yucatec social organization simply cannot be understood properly without examining the ways children participate in the culture.[12]

My own study of the North American "children's cult," to borrow a phrase from Anthony F. C. Wallace,[13] boldly underscores the autonomous impact children have in modern-day American cultural contexts. Understanding Easter, Christmas, or the Tooth Fairy ritual—and no doubt numerous cultural events in contemporary America—requires a full accounting of children's activity and perspectives.

## THE NATURE OF IMAGINAL EXPERIENCE

Santa, the Fairy, and the Bunny visit at night, of course. This timing may be surprising, given that children are usually inactive (indeed are asleep) at night. But, as natives explain, sleep is a time for dreaming, when, it is said, you "let your mind go." And night is a time when the ineffable, the uncanny, and a sense of dreamlike mystery, secretiveness, and magic descend.

Despite the apparently motionless state of juvenile slumberers, they do take action in three ways. First, they must "take action" by remaining asleep, suspended in dreams, for each of these mythic figures to visit. "If you're awake, he/she won't come" is the stated principle. Second, prior good behavior can be a condition of delivery, especially for Santa Claus or the Bunny. Third, and perhaps most telling, the familiar refrain that "he/she only comes if you believe" (a widespread idea) requires children to accept an unseen reality without conditions of patent proof.

Mothers commented that it is important for children to be able to accept nonlogical truths, sight unseen. This capacity is felt necessary for religious faith, for gaining access to transcendent reality.

> I think it's kind of nice . . . for them to believe in something they can't see. . . . If you really think about it logically, you know it can't happen. But it's kind of nice, it's fun to have them . . . believe in something they can't see and something they've never really seen. When they see Santa, they know that's not the real one . . . but as far as the real, real one . . .

> It probably ties over into the religious aspect, that there are things that you have to believe in that you can't always prove. And maybe [the Easter Bunny] is teaching them to accept things without asking questions sometimes.

> The parent might tell them . . . it's not a real thing. And we didn't want you to believe in something that wasn't real. But then, might they not believe in other things that they can't prove their existence? Like prayer and God and everything else? . . . If a parent says, we didn't want you to believe in that

kind of stuff because it's not real, how about other things that we take on faith?

The value placed on faith by mothers is not shared by all, of course. Cognitively oriented psychologists have very often treated imaginal belief as a primitive function (secondary to logical cognition) that distorts reality by putting the fantasizer out of touch with the way the world really is.[14] Like religious fundamentalists, such psychologists share an assumption that reality is singular and that representing reality is a straightforward process with only one right answer. For instance, it is often presupposed in developmental psychological research that if children make differing reality judgments than adults (e.g., treat Mickey Mouse or the Teenage Mutant Ninja Turtles as "real"), this is due to their lack of competence in the proper evaluative procedures[15] for judging reality. By this view, adults are simply more competent than children at detecting reality, a reality assumed to singularly adhere directly to the text or entity in question.

To assume that certain cultural entities are inherently real, however, and that normal adults uniformly apply the correct schema for detecting this reality, ignores the unfixed, dynamic nature of the process by which reality is socially constituted. Adults have been known to treat fictional media characters as reified figures: Figures (from Elvis to June Cleaver) are used as mentors and role models and thereby have effects on actual adult social relationships.[16] Robert Young, who played the physician Marcus Welby on the TV show, received some five thousand letters a week asking for medical advice.[17] Adults (and children too) are inextricably part of the process by which ongoing, shared cultural reality is continually co-constructed.

Further, culture provides many instances of objects fanciful, mythological, and religious that defy single-encoded meanings, that conflate notions of fantasy and reality, that are ambiguous and incongruous, that are "unpetrified" texts embodying shifting perspectives and multiplicity.[18] Developing members of a culture must learn to take meaning from such elusive, multifaceted entities.

The rite of passage by which American children give up literal belief in Santa or the Tooth Fairy or the Easter Bunny provides them with an exercise in navigating just such ambiguous, unpetrified beings. Children gradually come to know that there are representations involved in such objects, and that the "real" Santa (or Bunny or Fairy) is actually unseen (in normal circumstances) and lacking in patent material presence. In other words, older children appreciate the distinction between concrete symbols and the referential, transcendent meaning behind those symbols. As early as age six or seven, most children treated the shopping mall impersonator as a masked referent, a mere representation of the real Santa. This was not seen as misleading or dishonest, but simply a case of an actor acting as if he or she were Santa or the Bunny. As Joseph Campbell has written, culture "can teach us to go past its concepts."[19] The more Santa becomes treated as a representation (and not a literal reality), the more the underlying essence (rather than the mask) leaps forward.

The subtle paradox entailed in this mental leap is similar to the paradox of play discussed by Gregory Bateson.[20] Bateson posited that signals are framed by metacommunicative messages that contextualize or "frame" contained communication. In Bateson's scheme, primary-process thought (where Bateson located religion) denies the difference between sign and referent, between map and territory—such that a flag is worth dying for, in and of itself. In secondary-process thought, map and territory are discriminated, sign and referent treated as separate. In play, finally (as in imaginal thought, as I conceive it), a paradox is at work, in that map and territory are simultaneously equated and discriminated. Whether an interaction is framed by an understanding that "this is play" will affect the psychological construction of the contained material as fanciful or objectively real or as simultaneously both. Play involves the kind of paradox entailed in a statement I've heard from a storyteller: "This is a true story. It may even have happened." The fundamental truth of the story is affirmed, yet simultaneously its literal reality is up for grabs.

In some respects, using the word *object* to refer to such entities as fairies is to misappropriate the word. *Objective reality* implies a reality external to the person experiencing it. If the figures in the children's cult are objects at all, they are objects in a different sense, transitional objects, which are simultaneously objective and subjective.

D. W. Winnicott used the term transitional object to refer to the thing or object of attachment that Charlie Brown's friend Linus (of the *Peanuts* cartoon strip) labeled his "security blanket." It could also be a teddy bear, rag doll, or other beloved possession. The transitional object belongs to an intermediate area of experiencing, to which inner reality and external life both contribute.[21] This transitional space is interactive, unstereotypical, maneuverable, and variable. The child neither complies nor acquiesces when incorporating a cultural symbol into the transitional sphere, but rather creatively reaches out and incorporates the symbol into a "neutral area of experience which will not be challenged."[22] Art and religion, in Winnicott's account, lie within this intermediate "resting place" that gives pleasurable "relief" from the strain of relating inner (personal) and outer (shared) experience. Reality claims are irrelevant within this transitional space, derived from the imaginative, metaphorical play of childhood. However, the experience may be shared, in that cultural members may find "a degree of overlapping" in the content of their transitional spheres.[23] For instance, individuals with similar beliefs (e.g., shared belief in the coming apocalypse, or in the immortality of Elvis) may experience a social sharing of transitional space. Families, too, as we have seen in prior chapters, may participate in ritual acts that conspire to preserve the quasi-sacred (or sacred) entities within their children's imaginal make-believe.[24] For example, bedtime rituals might include an imaginal companion who is bid good night along with the child; Christmas rituals might accommodate an imaginal red-nosed reindeer, for whom carrots are left. Children who bring toys to life often do so in collaboration with siblings or with other children: The young Brontës (before growing up to be literary figures) involved their enlivened toy soldiers in jointly created elaborate adventures in Africa, even writing books and magazines for them.[25]

Winnicott's notion of interpersonally overlapping transitional space honors fairies and holiday spirits with the "incontestable value" of transitional objecthood. The issue of detecting reality ultimately is rephrased and overhauled within such a framework. Rather than reality per se, the issue involves the "overlap in the common experience" of culture members—who may either coincide or differ (or perhaps both coincide and differ) in what they include within their respective transitional spheres.

Although transitional space can be interpersonally shared, it is not constraining. Objects within this realm are uniquely playful and versatile. Transitional objects are also apt to be steeped in paradoxical ambiguity. A mutual suspension of disbelief is required for culture members to relate to transitional objects.

Metaphor is an important conceptual mechanism involved in transitional space, I would assert. Metaphor is creative rather than constraining, in that the allusive ties or common attributes implied by metaphor are discoverable by the individual, rather than literal and explicit.[26] Metaphor allows one person to focus on a particular aspect of a symbol (that fairies are associated with early childhood), while another person focuses on a quite different aspect (that money brought by fairies confers maturity). Metaphor is a construct used from an early age,[27] is both conceptual and linguistic,[28] used in pretend play, and is a common mechanism behind cultural symbols.

As long as symbols are treated metaphorically rather than literally, it is possible for symbols to be shared without placing "challenging claims" on one another.

Aside from metaphor, narrative may also be a structure that helps to more deeply involve a person with imaginal experience. Paul Pruyser has illustrated this in discussing fairy tales:

> Unlike cautionary tales and direct moralizations, fairy tales have the grace to let a child find his own solutions to his existential problems, at his own pace, and by as many rereadings and retellings as necessary. Fairy tale themes are to be mulled over: now this, now that aspect of a story will register.[29]

Structures such as metaphor and narrative are valuable in constructing shared transitional space precisely because they give leeway to the individual in imputing meaning. Consider that condensed cultural symbols—condensed in the sense of providing a richness of variegated, even paradoxical implications—will be particularly conducive to shared meaningfulness: The significance imputed by each individual at a particular time will be uniquely derived, yet the richness of meaning allows for a broad sharing of imaginal involvement.

According to Winnicott's theory of transitional space, an emotional component—trust—is also essential to the relaxed, creative experience that enables the "use of symbols that stand at one and the same time for external world phenomena and for phenomena of the individual person."[30] Ultimately, mythological experience is made possible by the capacity for trust (without which the suspension of disbelief is inhibited). Trust has been said by other theorists to be a prime precursor to faith in God. It is trust that enables an active engagement between child and imaginal object, thereby giving vitality to the mythic entity.[31] Said another way, it is the child's active, presuming belief that gives life to the imaginal object; this, of course, further supports the idea that myth and ritual are not just passively received ("*socialized*") but rather actively constituted by the child.

It has been theorized that a lack of trust, making faith more difficult, can be traced to early family relationships.[32] A troubled family interviewed during this study lends support to the idea that family milieu can either contribute to or detract from trust, as necessary for faith. This family, the Heinzes, is atypical of the families interviewed. But their very exceptionality is illuminating.

The Heinzes lived in a working-class neighborhood, in a home located (ironically perhaps) just around the corner from a candy factory. Mrs. Heinz is the daughter of immigrants. (The family is of German-Polish extraction.) Mr. Heinz has a high school education and works for the fire department.

When I visited them a few days after Christmas, I noticed that their home stood out from the other houses on the block. The Christmas decorations were relatively modest: snowflake cutouts on the windows, a simple wreath on the door. Regardless, the yuletide decorations were barely noticeable, overshadowed by what made the house so striking among its neighbors in this holiday season: a major part of the facade was covered by two flags, an enormous American flag and a black banner honoring American military POWs/MIAs.

Mrs. Heinz greeted me at the door, and her two sons (ages six and eleven) played in their bedroom while I talked with her at the kitchen table. One quickly sensed that this was a troubled family. Mrs. Heinz mentioned that her husband was a "former alcoholic." She reported that when Hank (the six-year-old) was a baby, she and Mr. Heinz were "having some problems in our marriage." She saw a preacher on television one day and heard him say, "If you've got any problems, give it to the foot of the Cross." She explained her dramatic reaction. "I just said, 'I can't take this any more. I messed up my life. You know, here, you take it.' And since then, my life has changed dramatically."

Mrs. Heinz had been raised Catholic but had no inner fulfill-ment from that tradition. As she put it, the "Catholic church, they just have their same old mundane thing every Sunday, and I just wasn't getting no inner feeling. They sing jolly old songs, they sound dead." As a result, Mrs. Heinz went "searching": "I started searching, and I started reading the Bible and, where do I go now? So I go to a full Gospel church where they really teach the Bible."

Exposed to Bible "teachings," Mrs. Heinz believed in the Bible literally, as proven historical fact. Rather than an imaginal, transi-tional entity, Bible learning was to her strictly factual. In fact, her children had "Bible quizzes" each Sunday in their church Sunday school program. Both boys had received Bibles as Christmas gifts.

Some aspects of secular Christmas were acceptable to Mrs. Heinz: a lighted Christmas tree—meaning, to her, everlasting life and the "light of the world"; and an extended family gathering on Christmas Day (which her husband did not attend because of his work schedule), complete with a video songfest. But she drew the line at Santa Claus. Mr. Heinz had taken the kids to a shop-ping center to see Santa in past years, but Mrs. Heinz had not been involved in the visit. She felt that Santa Claus was a lie—and worse, was credited for gifts and blessings that would be better credited to "the Lord." ("Christmas is the day we celebrate the

Lord's birthday. We shouldn't focus too much on Santa Claus.")
She viewed Santa Claus as the man at the mall who gives out
coloring books or little toys, no more, no less.

> Well, I think what people mostly want to try to do is use Santa
> Claus as the spirit of giving out gifts. But actually the spirit of
> giving isn't from Santa Claus, if you think about it. The spirit
> of giving is from the Lord. And so, he doesn't really give gifts
> out. Well, he gives out a coloring book or a little toy, but as
> far as your real gifts that . . . the kids ask for, they don't get
> it from Santa Claus. They find out that it's not from him. . . .
> I think it's kind of devastating to them, because, here, for
> however many years, they've been learning about Santa Claus,
> and they find out that he's not real. So I just think when they're
> ready to know the truth I'm gonna give it to 'em.

Listening to Mrs. Heinz, I realized that she equated the representation and the thing represented, noting no difference between the
sign and the referent. Such primary-process thought, in Bateson's
model, was an exception to the pattern of most informants, even
children. Because truth was literal and not in any sense meta-
phoric to her, only one symbolic world was possible for her ("the
Lord"). Those worshiping any other way—Buddhists, Hindus, or
children who believed in Santa Claus—were engaged in idolatry,
the worship of statues. To Mrs. Heinz, the world broke down
into facts and lies, and Santa Claus fell into the lie category, since
truth was singular. This is why, she said, she had decided to tell
Hank the truth, without hedging and sidestepping as most mothers did, when he began to ask clarifying questions.

> When my children asked me . . . I thought, I'm not gonna lie
> to him. 'Cause I want him to trust me. I don't want him to
> find out I'm lying to him. So I told him the truth. There isn't
> . . . I just want him to trust me . . . when he gets older and
> not [be] thinking I'm gonna lie to him. Because I just don't
> care to do that. I'd been lied to when I was little. And I found
> out, I was devastated. [CDC: About Santa Claus?] No, no, no.
> But little things your parents will tell you just to kinda cover

up things, or something. It's like, well can I trust them? You know? It can do some damage.

Mrs. Heinz felt so strongly about these issues that she kept on hand a supply of leaflets discussing Christmas and depicting Santa Claus as a sad figure at the foot of a crucifix. She pushed one of these into my hands, to keep.

Trust (or better said, lack of trust) was a key dilemma for Mrs. Heinz. She saw her search for true faith as a solution to a lack of parental love in her childhood, since it provided an inner power, an inner security that she lacked. The contention that trust enables transitional space, and that there is a bridge from the transitional object to religious experience, provides an apt explanatory template for Mrs. Heinz's fundamentalism. Out of a lack of trust, she struggled (with some desperation) to find a proven truth. Suspension of disbelief was not an experience for which she was well prepared.

Like many psychoanalysts,[33] but in contrast to most mothers, Mrs. Heinz felt that Santa Claus was a harmful lie that itself threatened a child's trust. Her metaphor for this (echoing Winnicott) was that taking away Santa Claus once a child believed in him was like taking away a child's teddy bear.

> It's like if somebody, a little kid, had a teddy bear, and he grew up with it for a while, and then all of a sudden you just took that teddy bear away and said, "Well, you shouldn't be doing this. This isn't real life." . . . You know what I'm saying? I mean, that can be devastating to some children, maybe not to others.

It is ironic, indeed, that Mrs. Heinz sympathizes with children who are abruptly deprived of imaginal figures. For according to Hank's account, his mother was abrupt and dramatic when she told him that Santa was a lie. Hank's portrayal of events was far harsher than I'd expected, given his mother's comments.

> HANK (broad smile, smug tone): I know Santa Claus is fake.
> . . .
> CDC: You look so proud of yourself that you know that. How did you find out, Hank, that Santa Claus was a fake?

HANK: Because my mom went upstairs and she [giggle]—
scared to say. [Pauses, then speaks.] She asked Jesus if Santa
Claus was fake or not, and he said, "Change the words
around." And she changed it, and it said "Satan." . . .

CDC: Um, why are you scared to say that?

HANK: Because, saying about Jesus.

CDC: You're scared to say "Jesus."

HANK: No, just scared. That's all [giggles]. Don't know . . .

CDC: Who is Jesus, can you explain that to me?

HANK: He knows everything. He knows what you're doing,
and he knows what to do and everything. [Pause.] And when
. . . you could go to heaven or hell.

CDC: Mm-hmm, where do you think most people go?

HANK: Mm, to hell.

CDC: Really, why?

HANK: Because most people do bad.

Hank went on to explain to me that Santa (that is, Satan) is
the force that makes people do bad. Since learning about the
Santa-Satan connection from his mother, Hank had been smugly
telling everyone that Santa Claus is fake. In fact, his teacher had
called Mrs. Heinz and expressed concern about Hank's behavior.
It seems that one day in the classroom, Hank's teacher had asked
the children to draw Santa Claus to decorate paper bags, as con-
tainers for candy to be given at a party, and Hank refused: "I
went to my teacher and I said, 'I can't make Santa Claus. Because
my ma said.'"

Yet during my interview with Hank, he willingly drew Santa
for me, twice, to give me a better idea of what most people
thought about Santa Claus. Hank felt that both adults and children usually believe in Santa Claus. He did not see his lack of
belief as a badge of maturity (as some children do), since he did
not feel that belief in Santa was age graded.

Hank described Santa's personality as "nice" and drew his face
as smiling and pleasant. Yet this depiction contradicted Hank's
repeated insistence that Santa Claus is "bad" and belongs in hell,
because "he makes people think he's real, and he's like making
a lie."

Ironically, whereas Hank was familiar with aspects of the Santa Claus myth (for example, Rudolph), he was totally unable to explain why Christmas is celebrated or to tell me anything about the religious narrative of Christmas. Even when I probed very directly ("Is Christmas someone's birthday?"), he gave me no sign that he had any awareness of the Nativity ("No"). He "forgot" if they ever talked about Christmas at Sunday school.

Hank gave a clear impression of being conflicted over the issue of Santa Claus: His mother had driven home the message that Santa was in the same league as Satan, but this did not leave Hank with any alternative symbolic depiction of Christmas. When asked what he liked about Christmas, Hank was strictly material-istic. He liked the presents. He was willing to admit that he liked the tangible gift (a coloring book) that the shopping center Santa had given him. But no transcendent meaning to Christmas was salient for him.

The Heinz family was aberrant in its Christmas ritual. Notably, theirs was a ritual in which trust played less part than fear. When the playful customs of Christmas were severed by Hank's mother as something satanic, something deeper seemed to be severed in the process. She had emphasized what *not* to believe, which seemed to undermine the proclivity to believe anything at all. Hank derived neither comfort nor joy from either of the age-graded traditions of Christmas: the adult mythology of the Nativ-ity, or the juvenile mythology of Santa Claus.

That Mrs. Heinz likened the process of belief and disbelief to a transitional object, the teddy bear, holds an interpretive key for what had gone so differently in this family than in others. Her jealousy of the children's myth, which threatened her own, per-haps tenuous, adult mythology, led Mrs. Heinz to seize control over the direction of Hank's trust. In the end, she accomplished just the opposite of what she intended. Without autonomous, free, creatively enacted trust, transitional space lacks a basis for *any* comfort-giving myth—either child oriented or adult oriented.

Members of a pluralistic society benefit from a capacity for faith, without the expectation that their version of imaginal reality will be universally endorsed. Faith involves mutual tolerance. On the one hand, there can be common experience that allows for the sharing of transitional space among mutual believers. But on the other hand, challenging claims placed on a person's imaginal experience, such as Mrs. Heinz placed on Hank's belief, can deaden the mythological imagination altogether, killing the capacity for faith.

Most mothers I interviewed were quite unlike Mrs. Heinz. Appreciation for the paradoxical qualities of the mythological imagination, which involves both subjective and objective aspects, was common among informants. To quote a more typical mother:

> After third grade . . . [my daughter] asked me about Santa Claus. And I said to her. . . , "It's all in what you want to believe. If you want to believe that there's a Santa Claus, there is one. If you don't want to believe there's a Santa Claus, well then, there's not. It's all what you have in your heart and how you feel." And I explained to her, the same with the Easter Bunny. . . . And I said. . . , "there's a lot of people who don't believe in God. It's all in what you want to believe. If you want to believe there's a God, there's a God. . . . And if you want to believe there's a Santa Claus, there really is." And they accepted it. That was the answer for them. They never questioned.

Mothers, by and large, sense an important and consequential principle that emerges as one of the key conclusions of this study: For faith to provide the sense of sacred sanctuary implicit to a vital mythology, the paradoxical interplay between subject and object is essential. In other words, the child (or adult for that matter) needs leeway to find their own faith, in their own way. For if cultural symbols are to be taken as self-evident, axiomatic sources of trust—as *real*—the process requires subject-object interplay within transitional space.

The transitional space, or imaginal experience, of the individual member of a culture makes myth and ritual possible, by providing "a resting-place for the individual engaged in the perpetual human task of keeping inner and outer reality separate but interrelated."[34] In a sense, it is precisely because children are autonomous cultural members who are able to actively reach out and adopt cultural content as their own that culture is able to remain vital and dynamic. Culture and child are mutually constituting.

This investigation reveals that, however children are taught by their elders, they resist some cultural content (e.g., certain aspects of religious narratives), welcome some cultural innovations (e.g., Rudolph, for most children), and successfully introduce some cultural practices themselves (e.g., letters to the Tooth Fairy, egg coloring at Easter).

The artifacts of children's rituals may indeed be material in nature. Still, the capacities children exercise during these rituals are ultimately not material at all—but priceless nevertheless.

As Peter Pan once claimed, a new baby's first laugh caused the beginning of fairies. But unless children continue to believe, fairies die. Children, when they know how, have the active ability to make real those things in which they can find sanctuary and meaning. Through the reality-making power of imaginal experience, children influence ritual in their own right. Nothing less than faith and tolerance hang in the balance of the developmental process.

# Appendix

# Child Anthropology
## *A Methodological Discussion*

Trained in anthropology as well as developmental psychology, I have been amused when research sponsors or others call me by the title "child anthropologist." Hearing such a title, I have been known to smile with glee, imagining myself as a three-foot-tall minor (dressed in diminutive safari attire) whose youthful curiosity is aimed at studying some complex cultural rite. When all is said and done, though, there is a certain appeal to the title "child anthropologist." Perhaps children would be better respected in many instances if other children studied them, rather than superior-minded adults.

Quite often, the methodological approach taken when studying children's ideas reveals a bias toward labeling children as "immature" and therefore "unfinished, in process, not anywhere yet."[1] The problem of how children become members of a particular culture has too often been reduced to the question of how children acquire culture.[2] In this approach, the bias can be quite adultcentric. The very terms *development* and *socialization* belie a focus on what children are lacking, relative to adults. Children's views, such as assuming the reality of a Tooth Fairy or Easter Bunny, can be routinely discounted when they violate adult views. The issue of Santa Claus, when treated in an adultcentric manner, becomes a case of not yet distinguishing fantasy from reality. Adults, even adults who study children, too often ridicule children rather than take them seriously.

This issue of adultcentrism bears on conceptual thinking about research issues to be explored, for example, whether children's understanding of reality is taken as a given. Avoiding adultcentrism also relates directly to methodological issues: Ethnographers strive to retain their "genuine desire to learn the 'truth' of the informants' world as they define it,"[3] and the vigilance needed to be open to the child's perspective throughout research is marked. This includes being willing to put aside certain controlling, disciplinary behaviors that are common adult modes of interacting with children.[4] It includes being sensitive to the child's spontaneous discourse strategies and following the child's lead in conversation. It includes playing dumb at times so as to establish oneself as a naive investigator in need of guidance by the child, the reverse of the usual adult-child relationship.

In the interviews conducted for this study, I strove to be sensitive to children's language practices and their normal ways of sharing information with each other. There was great variation from child to child in the kinds of discourse strategies that worked best to draw out and explore the child's world. But there was a clear and distinct difference between the conduct of adult interviews, via question and answer, and the conduct of child interviews, which were filled with role-playing, picture drawing, prop use, and other gamelike strategies for communication. Communicative blunders can happen in an informant interview when questions are asked in a manner foreign to the group under study, an observation that applies to age group differences as much as cultural differences.[5]

For example, I like to use props and drawings in talking with young children because having an artifact to talk about duplicates the way in which one makes friends with a child in our society: A toy (the material prop) or some play activity is shared. A puppet figure of a toothless child was used with much success to find out what it's like to lose a tooth. "Bunny ears" were worn by many a young informant (or me), as the child acted out or instructed how the Easter Bunny behaved. Cutout pictures of Santa or various would-be Easter rabbits were sorted through to see which were right and wrong in children's eyes. As an example of how such stimuli helped children to communicate their perceptions of the Easter Bunny, note the following brief excerpt from a role-playing episode that lasted 130 conversational turns while the seven-year-old female informant wore rabbit ears.

> CDC: I'm gonna pretend you're the Easter Bunny. You're down there in your hole, and there's the grass. [CDC gestures playfully and describes action as does so:] Push the grass aside and yell down the hole. "Easter Bunny! Tell me, what do you do all day down in your hole?"
>
> GIRL: I work.
>
> CDC: What's your work? What kind of work do you do?
>
> GIRL: I paint eggs.
>
> CDC: Where do you get your eggs, Easter Bunny?
>
> GIRL: My chickens.
>
> CDC: You have chickens, too, oh my. Easter Bunny, I've always wanted to know how you got started bringing all that stuff for kids. What's the story of it? . . . Have you been doing it a long time or a short time?
>
> GIRL: A long time.
>
> CDC: How old are you?
>
> GIRL: A hundred.
>
> CDC: . . . You work a lot painting those eggs. I bet that's hard work. You don't have anybody to help you paint the eggs?
>
> GIRL: No.
>
> CDC: You do it all by yourself.
>
> GIRL: Yeah, but only my chicken lay the eggs.

The rationale for letting an informant interview take such a fanciful direction is to provide a communicative context compatible with native systems of communication within that age set, in this case children's role-playing. The playful *form* of the interview is a way to meet the goal of being open to the child's perspective.

Perhaps more important than any prop or game, however, is the attitude of listening to the child, treating the interview as a form of active listening that takes up a child's thought and pursues it farther, rather than pursuing the adult interviewer's line of thought. In other words, the child's frame of reference is taken seriously. Rather than using a structured or semistructured questionnaire, the principles of the focused interview were adopted.

The focused interview is aimed at allowing the interviewee to express what they have self-defined as important, rather than responding to an interviewer's definition of presumed importance.[6] Toward this end, an interview guide was prepared, with the goal of focusing the interview on the subjective experiences of the person to ascertain *their definitions of the situation*. The nondirective approach made the research compatible with the goals of child-centered research, with the guiding principle being to honor and understand the child's definition and understanding of the situation.

As an ethnographer studying children, I have discovered that they are in fact already somewhere, not just on their way to an adult destination, and, further, in a very interesting place indeed. Children have much to teach us. But we as adults have two initial lessons to learn. First, we must learn, in interviews, how to engage youthful interest in an appropriate way (playful methods or props, we have seen, work well). Second, we grown-ups must learn how to fully listen when our queries are rejoined, since children's perspectives may differ from ours.

## SPECIFIC STUDY DETAILS

The fieldwork included in this analysis began in September and December 1985, when myself and six other researchers[7] interviewed sixty-one middle-class suburban boys and girls between the ages of five and ten about Christmas and Santa Claus. The sample was balanced by age and gender. Half the interviews took place during September 1985 and the other half during December 1985. These first informant interviews were conducted in the brightly lit, informal rec room in an apartment building.

Subsequent interviews were conducted entirely by Cindy Clark, in the homes of the informants. Thirty-two families were interviewed during August–October 1988 about the Tooth Fairy ritual. In each family, the mother had indicated via a telephone recruiting survey that the interviewed child lost a tooth during the previous two weeks. The Chicago area families ranged from middle class to working class, and included both urban and suburban households. (Note that in one family of Jehovah's Witnesses, the Tooth Fairy ritual was not fully practiced because of their religious doctrine. The custom in this exceptional family was for the parents to directly pay their child a dollar for each lost tooth.) Mother and child were interviewed separately and privately (each out of hearing range of the other). There were fifteen boys and seventeen girls in the sample, which was roughly balanced by age to include children ages five, six, seven, and eight.

During 1989–90, three additional rounds of ethnographic data collection took place in the Chicago metropolitan area. First, interviews with mothers and children were conducted in households immediately following Christmas and Easter. The sample included forty children (ten boys and ten girls for Christmas and ten boys and ten girls for Easter), as well as their mothers. Again, mother and child were interviewed separately and privately. The sample was balanced by age and included children ages six and seven.

A second round of research in 1989–90 involved videotaped observation in a shopping mall in a Chicago suburb. This was a site where children "visit" Santa Claus or the Easter Bunny and are commercially photographed. To allow for videotaping children's visits, cooperation was obtained from a firm that hires, trains, and places costumed personnel to portray Santa or the Easter Bunny. The single mall location for the study was in a predominantly working-class suburb of Chicago and was frequented by a racially diverse population. As the principal investigator, I was aided in this portion of the study by a professional cameraman, who did the videotaping while I obtained informed consent from families who had just been videotaped. Videotapes were transcribed according to a protocol used by William Corsaro in his study of peer culture.[8] Particular behaviors of interest (crying and the like) were systematically coded from the videotape transcripts.

A third round of research in 1989–90 involved asking researcher-mothers to record field notes describing their children's behavior vis-à-vis Santa Claus, the Easter Bunny, and/or the Tooth Fairy. Six mothers recorded field notes from December 1, 1989 through May 31, 1990. Four of these researcher-recorders had research experience, and some of them were employed as professional researchers. Half of the mothers had at least a master's degree. All had at least one child aged six to seven at the time the record keeping began.

The procedure of asking mothers to record observations of their children's behavior has a precedent in Florence Good-enough's 1931 study of children's outbursts of anger.[9] The method has been used more recently by E. Mark Cummings, Carolyn Zahn-Waxler, and Marian Radke-Yarrow.[10] Of the techniques used, mothers' field notes perhaps came closest to approximating a classic ethnographer's relationship with informants that occurs over time. Mothers recorded data for a six-month period. These field notes provided repeated indications that children's involvement with Santa Claus or the Easter Bunny was not just a fleeting occurrence for holiday time only. Even when no gifts were immediately at stake, children warmly related to these holiday icons.

> I handed [my daughter] a doll she'd gotten from Santa last year (1988) to sleep with. She spontaneously said (remembering it had been from Santa), "I love Santa Claus." I asked why she said that. "Because he gives such nice presents." [Maternal Field Notes, 1/18/90]

> Today [my son] said (while we were brushing our teeth) something like this:
>
> SON (age five): Mom, do you know Santa's sleigh that flied in the air is fun?
> MOTHER: Yes.
> SON: It only flied with reindeer. I would like to ride in that sleigh just once.
> MOTHER: I would too. That would be neat, wouldn't it?
> SON: Yep. [Maternal Field Notes 1/29/90]

At times mothers offered me a (written) interpretation of an event that happened, just as a conventional ethnographic informant might. One mother recorded a conversation with her seven-year-old son:

> SON: You know mom when I get my proton pack that's new—
> MOTHER: What proton pack?
> SON: The one I asked Santa for—

> Just a conversation that started but never finished. Only for illustration purposes that he still believes that Santa does grant what children want.

I suspect that written field notes kept by mothers reflected their personal degree of involvement with the custom under study. The mother who was least involved in or endorsing of Santa Claus or the Easter Bunny kept field notes that were quite sparse, in contrast to mothers who endorsed the Santa Claus or Easter Bunny custom. The notes of the latter group tended to be longer, more detailed, and more full of commentary. Unlike traditional ethnographic fieldwork, where the long-term informant is apt to be a "marginal" individual, willing to get involved with an outsider and comment on his or her own customs from a detached stance, this research was an intracultural investigation of customs that were highly significant to the informants. Natives, asked to keep written field notes for an inquirer within their own culture, tended to provide more in-depth information when they themselves were deeply involved in the customs being studied.

Laid over all the forms of data collection—informant interviews, mother's field notes, and direct observation—were my own second-order interpretations. Despite my native membership in the culture being studied (as an American mother of a young child), I am by professional habit a practiced interpreter of American child culture. I know well what Fine asserts, that adults are apt to presume that they know more about children's culture than they actually do,[11] overstating what the mature have learned by passing through childhood in the past. Child-centered research forever reminds me how easy it is for adults to misunderstand or to remember strangely in the odd glow of hindsight. I have had the experience of being set straight many times.

I do not promise that child-centered research provides a firsthand return to second childhood. Children are indeed "other"—a product of their own historical time and first-order experience of youth.[12] Still, studying children does awaken a deepened appreciation (and reframed understanding) of experiences long forgotten by the supposedly older and wiser. It is in this spirit that this book and its interpretations are presented for the adult reader.

# Notes

## CHAPTER ONE

1. Judith Boss, "Is Santa Corrupting Our Children?" *Free Inquiry* 11, no. 4 (1991): 27.

2. Robert Coles, *The Spiritual Life of Children* (Boston: Houghton Mifflin, 1990).

3. D. W. Winnicott, *Playing and Reality* (London: Tavistock Publications, 1971).

4. J. M. Barrie, *Peter Pan* (New York: Henry Holt, 1987), 25.

5. Paul Veyne, *Did the Greeks Believe in Their Myths?* (Chicago: University of Chicago Press, 1988).

## CHAPTER TWO

1. Theodore Ziolkowski, "The Telltale Teeth: Psychodontia to Sociodontia," *PMLA* 91 (1976): 9–22.

2. H. S. Darlington, "The Tooth-Losing Dream," *Psychoanalytic Review* 29 (1942): 71–79; Jackson Steward Lincoln, *The Dream in Primitive Cultures* (London: Cresset Press, 1935; New York: Johnson Reprint Corp., 1970).

3. Sandor Lorand, "On the Meaning of Losing Teeth in Dreams," *Psychoanalytic Quarterly* 17 (1948): 529–30; Sandor Lorand and Sandor Feldman, "The Symbolism of Teeth in Dreams," *International Journal of Psychoanalysis* 36 (1955): 145–61; Jerome Schneck, "Loss of Teeth in Dreams Symbolizing Fear of Aging," *Perceptual and Motor Skills* 24 (1967): 792, and "Total Loss of Teeth in Dreams," *American Journal of Psychiatry* 112 (1956): 939.

4. Sigmund Freud, *The Interpretation of Dreams,* trans. James Strachey (New York: Avon Books, 1965).

5. William Carter, Bernard Butterworth, and Joseph Carter, *Ethnodentistry and Dental Folklore* (Kansas City, KS: Dental Folklore Books of Kansas City, 1987), 77.

6. "Attitude toward and Special Treatment of Developmental Events," Human Relations Area Files, Topical Classification no. 856.

7. Joyce Robertson, "A Mother's Observations of the Tonsillectomy of Her Four Year Old Daughter (with Commentary by Anna Freud)," *Psychoanalytic Study of the Child* 11 (1956): 410–33.

8. T. J. Scheff, *Catharsis in Healing, Ritual, and Drama* (Berkeley and Los Angeles: University of California Press, 1979).

9. Rosemary Wells, "The Tooth Fairy, Part II," *Cal Magazine*, February 1980, 18–24.

10. Sudir Kakar, *Shamans, Mystics, and Doctors* (Boston: Beacon Press, 1982).

11. John Silvestro, "Second Dentition and School Readiness," *New York State Dental Journal* 43, no. 3 (1977): 155–58.

12. Barbara Rogoff et al., "Age of Assignment of Roles and Responsibilities in Children: A Cross-Cultural Survey," *Human Development* 18, no. 5 (1975): 354.

13. Arnold Van Gennep, *The Rites of Passage* (Chicago: University of Chicago Press, 1960).

14. John O'Connor and Aaron Hoorwitz, "Imitative and Contagious Magic in the Therapeutic Use of Rituals with Children," in *Rituals in Families and Family Therapy,* ed. Evan Imber-Black, Janine Roberts, and Richard Whiting (New York: W. W. Norton, 1988), 135–37.

15. Stuart Albert et al., "Children's Bedtime Rituals as a Prototype Rite of Safe Passage," *Journal of Psychological Anthropology* 2, no. 1 (1979): 85–105.

16. Van Gennep, *The Rites of Passage,* xvii.

## CHAPTER THREE

1. To be sure, there are other holidays celebrated at roughly the same time of year as Christmas in contemporary America, for example, Hanukkah and the African American Kwanza festival. Since these festivals are less a part of the mainstream culture than the celebration of Christmas, these subcultural festivals are considered to be beyond the scope of this book. Another holiday that might be included in the annual cycle of children's festivals, but that is not treated in the present research is Halloween. For background on Halloween customs see Ralph Linton and Adelin Linton, *Halloween* (New York: Henry Schuman, 1950); and Russell Belk, "Halloween: An Evolving American Consumption Ritual," in *Advances in Consumer Research,* vol. 17, ed. Marvin Goldberg, Gerald Gorn, and Richard Polley (Provo, Utah: Association for Consumer Research, 1990).

2. E. O. James, *Seasonal Feasts and Festivals* (New York: Barnes and Noble, 1961); Robert Myers, *Celebrations: The Complete Book of American Holidays* (Garden City, N.Y.: Doubleday, 1972).

3. Alan Watts, *Easter: Its Story and Meaning* (London: Abelard-Schuman, 1950).

4. W. Lloyd Warner, *The Living and the Dead: A Study of the Symbolic Life of Americans* (New Haven: Yale University Press, 1959); W. Lloyd Warner, *The Family of God: A Symbolic Study of Christian Life in America* (New Haven: Yale University Press, 1961).

5. Sir James Frazer, *The Golden Bough: A Study in Magic and Religion* (London: Macmillan, 1915), 9:328.

6. Myers, *Celebrations.*

7. Ibid.; John Layard, *The Lady of the Hare: Being a Study in the Healing Power of Dreams* (London: Faber & Faber, 1943); Watts, *Easter.*

8. Diana Carey and Judy Large, *Festivals, Family, and Food* (Gloucestershire: Hawthorne Press, 1982), 16.

9. John F. Baldovin, "Easter," in *The Encyclopedia of Religion*, ed. Mircea Eliade (New York: Macmillan, 1987).

10. Cynthia Scheibe, "Developmental Differences in Children's Reasoning about Santa Claus and Other Fantasy Characters" (Ph.D. diss., Cornell University, 1987).

11. James Barnett, *The American Christmas: A Study in National Culture* (New York: Macmillan, 1954).

12. E. Wilbur Bock, "The Transformation of Religious Symbols: A Case Study of St. Nicholas," *Social Compass* 19 (1972): 537–48.

13. Myers, *Celebrations*, 312.

14. Barnett, *The American Christmas*, 5.

15. Myers, *Celebrations*.

16. Hutton Webster, "Rest Days: A Sociological Study," *University Studies* 11 (1911): 156–58.

17. Barnett, *The American Christmas*, 24.

18. Martin Ebon, *Saint Nicholas: Life and Legend* (New York: Harper & Row, 1975).

19. Charles Jones, *Saint Nicholas of Myra, Bari, and Manhattan* (Chicago: University of Chicago Press, 1978), 329.

20. Adrianus De Groot, *Saint Nicholas: A Psychoanalytic Study of His History and Myth* (The Hague: Mouton, 1965), 21.

21. Myers, *Celebrations*.

22. Barnett, *The American Christmas*, 26–27.

23. Quoted in Jones, *Saint Nicholas*, 347.

24. Ibid.

25. Barnett, *The American Christmas*.

26. Myers, *Celebrations*, 321.

27. Barnett, *The American Christmas*.

28. Philippe Ariès, *Centuries of Childhood* (New York: Vintage Books, 1962), 359.

29. Brian Sutton-Smith, *Toys as Culture* (New York: Gardner Press, 1986), 18–19.

30. Samuel Preston, "The Vanishing American Family: A Demographer's Perspective," *Penn Arts and Sciences*, Spring 1990, 8.

31. Barnett, *The American Christmas*, 109.

32. Ibid.

33. Ibid., 111.

34. Theodore Caplow, "Christmas Gifts and Kin Networks," *American Sociological Review* 47 (1982): 383–92, and "Rule Enforcement without Visible Means: Christmas Gift Giving in Middletown," *American Journal of Sociology* 89, no. 6 (1984): 1306–23; Theodore Caplow, Howard Bahr, and Bruce Chadwick, *All Faithful People: Change and Continuity in Middletown's Religion* (Minneapolis: University of Minnesota Press, 1983); Theodore Caplow et

al., *Middletown Families: Fifty Years of Change and Continuity* (Minneapolis: University of Minnesota Press, 1982); Theodore Caplow and Margaret Holmes Williamson, "Decoding Middletown's Easter Bunny: A Study in American Iconography," *Semiotica* 32 (1980): 221–32.

35. Caplow et al., *Middletown Families*, 234.

36. Ibid., 235.

37. Caplow, "Rule Enforcement"; Caplow, Bahr, and Chadwick, *All Faithful People*, 188.

38. Elizabeth Hirschman and Priscilla LaBarbara, "The Meaning of Christmas," in *Interpretive Consumer Research*, ed. Elizabeth Hirschman (Provo, Utah: Association for Consumer Research, 1989), 143.

39. Eileen Fischer, "'Tis the Season to Be Jolly? Tensions and Trends in Christmas Shopping" (paper presented at the annual meeting of the Association for Consumer Research, New Orleans, 1989).

40. Caplow et al., *Middletown Families*, 383.

41. Russell Belk, "Materialism and the Modern U.S. Christmas," in Hirschman, *Interpretive Consumer Research*, 118, and "A Child's Christmas in America: Santa Claus as Deity, Consumption as Religion," *Journal of American Culture* 10 (1987): 87–100.

42. Hirschman and LaBarbara, "The Meaning of Christmas," 141.

43. L. Bryce Boyer, "Christmas 'Neurosis,'" *Journal of the American Psychoanalytic Association* 3 (1955): 467–88; James Cattell, "The Holiday Syndrome," *Psychoanalytic Review* 42 (1955): 39–43; George Pollock, "Temporal Anniversary Manifestations: Hour, Day, Holiday," *Psychoanalytic Quarterly* 40 (1971): 123–31; Renzo Sereno, "Some Observations on the Santa Claus Custom," *Psychiatry* 14 (1951): 387–96.

44. Cattell, "The Holiday Syndrome," 39.

45. Sereno, "Observations,"392–94.

46. E.g., Boyer, "Christmas Neurosis"; Sereno, "Observations."

47. James Bossard and Eleanor Boll, *Ritual in Family Living* (Philadelphia: University of Pennsylvania Press, 1950), 199.

48. Steven Zeitlin, Amy Kotkin, and Holly Cutting Baker, *A Celebration of American Family Folklore* (New York: Pantheon Books, 1982).

49. Bossard and Boll, *Ritual in Family Living,*18–19.

50. Zeitlin, Kotkin, and Baker, *Celebration of Folklore*, 165.

51. Warner, *Living and Dead.*

52. Caplow et al., *Middletown Families*; Hirschman and LaBarbara, "The Meaning of Christmas."

53. Sutton-Smith, *Toys as Culture,*17–18.

54. David Plath, "The Japanese Popular Christmas: Coping with Modernity," *Journal of American Folklore* 76 (1963): 313.

55. Belk, "Materialism," 119.

56. James Barnett, "The Easter Festival—a Study in Cultural Change," *American Sociological Review* 14 (1949): 62–70.

57. Ibid., 66.

58. Myers, *Celebrations,* 104.

59. Ibid.

60. Ibid., 110.

61. Edna Barth, *Lilies, Rabbits, and Painted Eggs: The Story of the Easter Symbols* (New York: Clarion Books, 1970); T. Sharper Knowlson, *The Origin of Popular Superstitions and Customs* (London: T. Werner Laurie, 1930); Myers, *Celebrations;* Venetia Newall, *An Egg at Easter: A Folkloric Study* (Bloomington: Indiana University Press, 1971); Watts, *Easter;* Layard, *Lady of the Hare;* Manabu Waida, "Rabbits," in Eliade, *The Encyclopedia of Religion.*

62. Knowlson, *Origin of Popular Superstitions,*36–37.

63. Watts, *Easter,* 28.

64. Myers, *Celebrations,* 111.

65. Ibid.

66. Newall, *An Egg at Easter,* 326.

67. Myers, *Celebrations;* Layard, *Lady of the Hare.*

68. Waida, "Rabbits."

69. American culture often makes little distinction between the hare and the rabbit. From a cultural standpoint, European lore attributed to hares is widely attributed by Americans just as much to rabbits. See *Man: Myth, and Magic: An Illustrated Encyclopedia of the Supernatural,* ed. Richard Cavendish (New York: Marshall Cavendish, 1970.), s.v. "Hare." The biological difference between hares and rabbits—hares build no nests and bear young less helpless than the young of rabbits—is not highly salient in America.

70. Caplow, Bahr, and Chadwick, *All Faithful People.*

71. Ibid.

72. Ibid., 193.

73. Caplow and Williamson, "Decoding Middletown's Easter Bunny."

74. Edmund Leach, "Anthropological Aspects of Language: Animal Categories and Verbal Abuse," in *Reader in Comparative Religion,* ed. William Lessa and Evon Vogt (New York: Harper & Row, 1964; reprint 1979), 153–66.

75. Caplow et al., *Middletown Families.*

76. Warner, *The Family of God,* 369–70.

77. Caplow, Bahr, and Chadwick, *All Faithful People,* 197.

78. Caplow and Williamson, "Decoding Middletown's Easter Bunny," 229.

## CHAPTER FOUR

1. Margaret Mead, "An Investigation of the Thought of Primitive Children, with Special Reference to Animism," *Journal of the Royal Anthropological Institute* 62 (1932): 184.

2. Carl Anderson, "On Discovering the Truth: Children's Reactions to the Reality of the Santa Claus Myth" (Ph.D. diss., University of Texas at Austin, 1987); Scheibe, "Developmental Differences."

3. Claude Lévi-Strauss, "Where Does Father Christmas Come From?" *New Society* 19 (1963): 6.

4. Mircea Eliade, *The Sacred and the Profane: The Nature of Religion* (New York: Harcourt Brace Jovanovich, 1959), 92.

5. See Bruno Bettelheim, *The Uses of Enchantment* (New York: Vintage Books, 1977); and Wendy Doniger O'Flaherty, "Inside and Outside the Mouth of God: The Boundary between Myth and Reality," *Daedalus* 109 (1980): 93–125, *Dreams, Illusions, and Other Realities* (Chicago: University of Chicago Press, 1984), and *Other People's Myths* (New York: Macmillan, 1988).

6. For an insightful treatment of how contemporary American adults do use imagination, see John Caughey, *Imaginary Social Worlds* (Lincoln: University of Nebraska Press, 1984).

7. John Sherry, "Gift Giving in Anthropological Perspective," *Journal of Consumer Research* 10 (1983): 157–68.

8. Barry Schwartz, "The Social Psychology of the Gift," *American Journal of Sociology* 73, no. 1 (1967): 4.

9. Donna Fisher-Thompson et al., "Sex-Role Orientations of Children and Their Parents: Relationship to the Sex-Typing of Christmas Toys" (paper presented at the sixtieth anniversary meeting of the Society for Research in Child Development, New Orleans, March 1993).

10. Scheibe, "Developmental Differences," 59.

11. Eliade, *Sacred and Profane*.

12. Russell Belk, Melanie Wallendorf, and John Sherry, "The Sacred and the Profane in Consumer Behavior: Theodicy on the Odyssey," *Journal of Consumer Research* 16 (1989): 10.

13. Roger Abrahams, "The Language of Festivals: Celebrating the Economy," in *Celebration: Studies in Festivity and Ritual,* ed. Victor Turner (Washington D.C.: Smithsonian Institution Press, 1982), 167–68.

14. Mircea Eliade, *Patterns in Comparative Religion* (New York: New American Library, 1958), 10.

15. Abrahams, "The Language of Festivals," 175–76.

16. David Elkind, *The Child's Reality: Three Developmental Themes* (Hillsdale, N.J.: Lawrence Erlbaum Associates, 1978), 35.

17. Gordon Allport, *The Individual and His Religion* (New York: Macmillan, 1950), 29.

18. Scheibe, "Developmental Differences," 131.

19. Carol Zaleski, *Otherworld Journeys: Accounts of Near-Death Experience in Medieval and Modern Times* (New York: Oxford University Press, 1987), 187.

## CHAPTER FIVE

1. Caplow, Bahr, and Chadwick, *All Faithful People;* Caplow and Williamson, "Decoding Middletown's Easter Bunny"; Caplow et al., *Middletown Families.*

2. Sherry Ortner, "Is Female to Male as Nature Is to Culture?" in *Woman, Culture, and Society,* ed. Michelle Zimbalist Rosaldo and Louise Lamphere (Stanford: Stanford University Press, 1974), 77–78.

3. Joseph V. Hickey, William E. Thompson, and Donald L. Foster, "Becoming the Easter Bunny: Socialization into a Fantasy Role," *Journal of Contemporary Ethnography* 17, no. 1 (1988): 78.

4. D. W. Winnicott, "Transitional Objects and Transitional Phenomena," in *Collected Papers* (New York: Basic Books, 1951; reprint 1958), 229–42.

5. Winnicott, "Transitional Objects," 231. See also Mary Watkins, *Invisible Guests: The Development of Imaginal Dialogues* (Hillsdale, N.J.: Analytic Press, 1986); and Caughey, *Imaginary Social Worlds.*

6. Zeitlin, Kotkin, and Baker, *Celebration of Folklore,* 136.

7. Mary Chase, *Harvey* (New York: Dramatists Play Service, 1944).

8. Within the family ritual of some American households, the family member who first says the words "rabbit rabbit" on the first day of the month will receive good luck that month.

9. See Belk, "Halloween: An Evolving American Consumption Ritual."

10. Hickey, Thompson, and Foster, "Becoming the Easter Bunny," 87.

11. Norman Prentice, Martin Manosevitz, and Laura Hubbs, "Imaginary Figures of Early Childhood: Santa Claus, Easter Bunny, and the Tooth Fairy," *American Journal of Orthopsychiatry* 48 (1978): 625.

12. See W. Nikola-Lisa, "The Cult of Peter Rabbit" (paper presented at a meeting of the Society for Popular Culture, Toronto, 1990). For a treatment of one boy's imaginal use of the Peter Rabbit story, see Peggy G. Miller et al., "Troubles in the Garden and How They Get Resolved: A Young Child's Transformation of His Favorite Story," in *Memory and Affect in Development,* ed. Charles A. Nelson (Hillsdale, N.J.: Lawrence Erlbaum Associates, 1993), 87–114.

13. Eliade, *Sacred and Profane.*

14. Winnicott, *Playing and Reality.*

15. Marion Milner, "D. W. Winnicott and the Two-way Journey," in *Between Reality and Fantasy: Transitional Objects and Phenomena,* ed. Simon Grolnick and Leonard Barkin (New York: Jason Aronson, 1978), 41.

16. Mihaly Csikszentmihalyi and Eugene Rochberg-Halton, *The Meaning of Things: Domestic Symbols and the Self* (Cambridge: Cambridge University Press, 1981), 184–87.

17. Caplow and Williamson, "Decoding Middletown's Easter Bunny," 229.

18. Mary Knapp and Herbert Knapp, *One Potato, Two Potato: The Secret Education of American Children* (New York: W. W. Norton, 1976), 220.

## CHAPTER SIX

1. Preston, "The Vanishing American Family." See also Stephanie Coontz, *The Way We Never Were* (New York: Basic Books, 1992), for a balancing view on the much discussed demise of the family.

2. Belk, Wallendorf, and Sherry, "Sacred and Profane."

3. Victor Turner, *The Forest of Symbols* (Ithaca: Cornell University Press, 1967), 30.

4. Cf. Caplow, "Rule Enforcement."

5. Csikszentmihalyi and Rochberg-Halton, *The Meaning of Things*, 220–21.

6. Bossard and Boll, *Ritual in Family Living*, 130.

7. Imber-Black, Roberts, and Whiting, *Rituals in Families*, 76.

8. Gananath Obeyesekere, *Medusa's Hair: An Essay on Personal Symbols and Religious Experience* (Chicago: University of Chicago Press, 1981), 99.

9. Shirley Park Lowry, *Familiar Mysteries: The Truth in Myth* (New York: Oxford University Press, 1982), 170–72.

10. Caplow, "Christmas Gifts," 391.

11. Irena Chalmers, *The Great Christmas Almanac* (New York: Viking Studio Books, 1988), 68.

12. Belk, "Child's Christmas in America," 91.

13. Blayne Cutler, "Here Comes Santa Claus (Again)," *American Demographics*, December 1989, 32.

14. Turner, *Celebration*, 24. See also Abrahams, "The Language of Festivals."

15. This act of generosity was not an isolated incident from my fieldwork. Intriguingly, one experimental study also indicates that first-grade children who were asked to tell stories about Santa Claus were more generous than control first-graders (telling stories about the Easter Bunny, or pets) in contributing to handicapped children. See David J. Dixon and Harry L. Hom, "The Role of Fantasy Figures in the Regulation of Young Children's Behavior: Santa Claus, the Easter Bunny, and Donations," *Contemporary Educational Psychology* 9 (1984): 14–18.

16. Ira Zepp, *The New Religious Image of Urban America: The Shopping Mall as Ceremonial Center* (Westminster, Md.: Christian Classics, 1986).

17. Mary Douglas, *Purity and Danger: An Analysis of the Concepts of Pollution and Taboo* (London: Ark Paperbacks, 1966; reprint 1985), 94.

18. Sally F. Moore and Barbara Meyerhoff, *Secular Ritual* (Amsterdam: Van Gorcum, 1977).

19. Belk, Wallendorf, and Sherry, "Sacred and Profane."

## CHAPTER SEVEN

1. Margaret Mead, *Blackberry Winter* (New York: Pocket Books, 1972), 307.

2. Martin Manosevitz, Norman Prentice, and Frances Wilson, "Individual and Family Correlates of Imaginary Companions in Preschool Children," *Developmental Psychology* 8, no. 1 (1973): 72–79.

3. Mary Renck Jalongo, "Imaginary Companions in Children's Lives and Literature," *Childhood Education* 60 (1984): 166–71.

4. Mackenzie Brooks and Don Knowles, "Parents' Views of Children's Imaginary Companions," *Child Welfare* 61 (1982): 25–32.

5. Caughey, *Imaginary Social Worlds*.

6. For similar hypotheses by past social scientists, see also Wendell Oswalt, "A Particular Pattern: Santa Claus," in *Understanding Our Culture: An Anthropological View* (New York: Holt, Rinehart and Winston, 1970), 10; and Eric Wolf, "Santa Claus: Notes on a Collective Representation," in *Process and Pattern in Culture,* ed. Robert Manners (Chicago: Aldine Publishing, 1964), 147–55. For a brief description of "cargo cults"—for example, the belief among early nineteenth-century Melanesians that ancestral spirits would deliver goods—see Edward Green, "Cargo Cults," in *Encyclopedia of Anthropology,* ed. David Hunter and Philip Whitten (New York: Harper & Row, 1976).

7. James T. Proctor, "Children's Reactions to Christmas," *Journal of the Oklahoma State Medical Association* 60 (1967): 653–59.

8. Zeitlin, Kotkin, and Baker, *Celebration of Folklore,* 169.

9. See, for example, Barry Glassner, "Kid Society," *Urban Education* 11 (1976): 5–22.

10. Peggy Miller and Lisa Hoogstra, "How to Represent the Native Child's Point of View: Methodological Problems in Language Socialization" (paper presented at the annual meeting of the American Anthropological Association, Washington D.C., 1989).

11. Suzanne Gaskins, Peggy J. Miller, and William A. Corsaro, "Theoretical and Methodological Perspectives in the Interpretive Theory of Culture," *New Directions for Child Development* 58 (1992): 5–23.

12. Suzanne Gaskins and John Lucy, "The Role of Children in the Production of Adult Culture: A Yucatec Case" (paper presented at the annual meeting of the American Ethnological Society, Philadelphia, 1987), 1.

13. Anthony F. C. Wallace, *Religion: An Anthropological View* (New York: Random House, 1966), 77–79.

14. W. George Scarlett and Dennie Wolf, "When It's Only Make-Believe: The Construction of a Boundary between Fantasy and Reality in Storytelling," *New Directions for Child Development* 6 (1979): 40.

15. For sources relating to reality-fantasy judgments about television, see Patricia Morison, Hope Kelly, and Howard Gardner, "Reasoning about the Realities of Television: A Developmental Study," *Journal of Broadcasting* 25 (1981): 229–41; John Condry and Sue Freund, "Discriminating Real from Make-Believe on Television: A Developmental Study" (paper presented at the biannual meeting of the Society for Research in Child Development, Kansas City, Mo., 1989); Cynthia Scheibe, "Learning the Categories of 'Real' and 'Make-Believe': A Developmental Study" (paper presented at the biannual meeting of the Society for Research in Child Development, Kansas City, Mo., 1989); Patricia Morison, Margaret McCarthy, and Howard Gardner, "Exploring the Realities of Television with Children," *Journal of Broadcasting* 23 (1979): 453–63; Bradley Greenberg and Byron Reeves, "Children and the Perceived Reality of Television," *Journal of Social Issues* 32 (1976): 86–97. Also see Patricia Morison and Howard Gardner, "Dragons and Dinosaurs: The Child's Capacity to Differentiate Fantasy from Reality," *Child Development* 49 (1978): 642–48.

16. Caughey, *Imaginary Social Worlds,* 243.

17. Todd Gitlin, "Television's Screens: Hegemony in Transition," in *American Media and Mass Culture: Left Perspectives,* ed. Donald Lazere (Berkeley and Los Angeles: University of California Press, 1987), 286.

18. Richard Shweder, "How to Look at Medusa without Turning to Stone," *Contributions to Indian Sociology* 21 (1987): 52–53.

19. Joseph Campbell, *The Power of Myth* (New York: Doubleday, 1988), 64–65.

20. Gregory Bateson, "A Theory of Play and Fantasy," in *Steps to an Ecology of the Mind* (New York: Chandler Publishing, 1972), 177–93.

21. Winnicott, *Playing and Reality,* 2.

22. Ibid.

23. Ibid., 14.

24. Paul Pruyser, *The Play of the Imagination: Toward a Psychoanalysis of Culture* (New York: International Universities Press, 1983), 58.

25. For a fictional treatment of the Brontë's imaginal toy soldiers, see Pauline Clark, *The Return of the Twelves* (New York: Putnam's, 1962; reprint New York: Dell Yearling Classic, 1986).

26. George Lakoff and Mark Johnson, *Metaphors We Live By* (Chicago: University of Chicago Press, 1980).

27. Ellen Winner, *The Point of Words: Children's Understanding of Metaphor and Irony* (Cambridge, Mass.: Harvard University Press, 1988), 131.

28. Robert Verbruge, "The Primacy of Metaphor in Development," *New Directions in Child Development* 6 (1979): 77–84.

29. Pruyser, *Play of Imagination,* 109.

30. Winnicott, *Playing and Reality,* 109.

31. David Heller, *The Children's God* (Chicago: University of Chicago Press, 1986), 141–42; Ana-Maria Rizzuto, *The Birth of the Living God: A Psychoanalytic Study* (Chicago: University of Chicago Press, 1979).

32. Heller, *The Children's God;* Rizzuto, *Birth.*

33. For example, Sereno, "Observations."

34. Winnicott, *Playing and Reality,* 2.

## APPENDIX

1. Frances Waksler, "Studying Children: Phenomenological Insights," *Human Studies* 9 (1986): 73.

2. Gaskins, Miller, and Corsaro, "Theoretical and Methodological Perspectives."

3. Julie Tammivaara and D. Scott Enright, "On Eliciting Information: Dialogues with Child Informants," *Anthropology and Education Quarterly* 17 (1986): 225.

4. Gary Alan Fine, *With the Boys: Little League Baseball and Preadolescent Culture* (Chicago: University of Chicago Press, 1987); Tammivaara and Enright, "On Eliciting Information."

5. Charles Briggs, *Learning How to Ask: A Sociolinguistic Appraisal of the*

*Role of the Interview in Social Science Research* (Cambridge: Cambridge University Press, 1986).

6. Robert K. Merton, Marjorie Fiske, and Patricia L. Kendall, *The Focused Interview: A Manual of Problems and Procedures,* 2d ed. (New York: Free Press, 1990).

7. I am grateful to the other interviewers, Carol Hartman, Darlene Miskovic, Elizabeth Monroe-Cook, Roxanne Pilat, Cathy Sweitzer, and Linda Troste.

8. William A. Corsaro, *Friendship and Peer Culture in the Early Years* (Norwood, N.J.: Ablex Publishing, 1985).

9. Florence Goodenough, *Anger in Young Children* (Minneapolis: University of Minnesota Press, 1931).

10. E. Mark Cummings, Carolyn Zahn-Waxler, and Marian Radke-Yarrow, "Developmental Changes in Children's Reactions to Anger in the Home," *Journal of Children Psychology and Psychiatry* 25 (1984): 63–74.

11. Fine, *With the Boys,* 243.

12. For a treatment of American childhood as reflecting the historical context, see Viviana Zelizer, *Pricing the Priceless Child: The Changing Social Value of Children* (New York: Basic Books, 1985); and Gary Alan Fine and Jay Mechling, "Minor Difficulties: Changing Children in the Late Twentieth Century" in *America at Century's End,* ed. Alan Wolfe (Berkeley and Los Angeles: University of California Press, 1991), 58–78.

# References

Abrahams, Roger. "The Language of Festivals: Celebrating the Economy." In *Celebration: Studies in Festivity and Ritual,* ed. Victor Turner, 161–77. Washington, D.C.: Smithsonian Institution Press, 1982.

Albert, Stuart, Terry Amgott, Mildred Krakow, and Howard Marcus. "Children's Bedtime Rituals as a Prototype Rite of Safe Passage." *Journal of Psychological Anthropology* 2, no. 1 (1979): 85–105.

Allport, Gordon. *The Individual and His Religion.* New York: Macmillan, 1950.

Anderson, Carl. "On Discovering the Truth: Children's Reactions to the Reality of the Santa Claus Myth." Ph.D. diss., University of Texas at Austin, 1987.

Ariès, Philippe. *Centuries of Childhood.* New York: Vintage Books, 1962.

"Attitude toward and Special Treatment of Developmental Events." Human Relations Area Files, Topical Classification no. 856. Regenstein Library, University of Chicago.

Baldovin, John F. "Easter." In *The Encyclopedia of Religion,* ed. Mircea Eliade. New York: Macmillan, 1987.

Barnett, James. *The American Christmas: A Study in National Culture.* New York: Macmillan, 1954.

———. "The Easter Festival—a Study in Cultural Change." *American Sociological Review* 14 (1949): 62–70.

Barrie, J. M. *Peter Pan.* New York: Henry Holt, 1987.

Barth, Edna. *Lilies, Rabbits, and Painted Eggs: The Story of the Easter Symbols.* New York: Clarion Books, 1970.

Bateson, Gregory. "A Theory of Play and Fantasy." In *Steps to an Ecology of the Mind.* New York: Chandler Publishing, 1972.

Belk, Russell. "A Child's Christmas in America: Santa Claus as Deity, Consumption as Religion." *Journal of American Culture* 10 (1987): 87–100.

———. "Halloween: An Evolving American Consumption Ritual." In *Advances in Consumer Research,* vol. 17, ed. Marvin Goldberg, Gerald Gorn, and Richard Polley, 508–17. Provo, Utah: Association for Consumer Research, 1990.

———. "Materialism and the Modern U.S. Christmas." In *Interpretive Consumer Research,* ed. Elizabeth Hirschman, 115–34. Provo, Utah: Association for Consumer Research, 1989.

Belk, Russell, Melanie Wallendorf, and John Sherry. "The Sacred and the Profane in Consumer Behavior: Theodicy on the Odyssey." *Journal of Consumer Research* 16 (1989): 1–38.

Bettelheim, Bruno. *The Uses of Enchantment*. New York: Vintage Books, 1977.

Bock, E. Wilbur. "The Transformation of Religious Symbols: A Case Study of St. Nicholas." *Social Compass* 19 (1972): 537–48.

*The Book of Easter*. New York: Macmillan, 1911; reprint Detroit: Singing Tree Press, 1971.

Boorstin, Daniel J. "Christmas and Other Festivals of Consumption." In *The Americans: The Democratic Experience*. New York: Random House, 1973.

Boss, Judith. "Is Santa Corrupting Our Children?" *Free Inquiry* 11, no. 4 (1991): 24–27.

Bossard, James, and Eleanor Boll. *Ritual in Family Living*. Philadelphia: University of Pennsylvania Press, 1950.

Boyer, L. Bryce. "Christmas 'Neurosis.'" *Journal of the American Psychoanalytic Association* 3 (1955): 467–88.

Briggs, Charles. *Learning How to Ask: A Sociolinguistic Appraisal of the Role of the Interview in Social Science Research*. Cambridge: Cambridge University Press, 1986.

Brooks, Mackenzie, and Don Knowles. "Parents' Views of Children's Imaginary Companions." *Child Welfare* 61 (1982): 25–32.

Campbell, Joseph. *The Power of Myth*. New York: Doubleday, 1988.

Caplow, Theodore. "Christmas Gifts and Kin Networks." *American Sociological Review* 47 (1982): 383–92.

———. "Rule Enforcement without Visible Means: Christmas Gift Giving in Middletown." *American Journal of Sociology* 89, no. 6 (1984): 1306–23.

Caplow, Theodore, Howard Bahr, and Bruce Chadwick. *All Faithful People: Change and Continuity in Middletown's Religion*. Minneapolis: University of Minnesota Press, 1983.

Caplow, Theodore, Howard Bahr, Bruce Chadwick, Reuben Hill, and Margaret Holmes Williamson. *Middletown Families: Fifty Years of Change and Continuity*. Minneapolis: University of Minnesota Press, 1982.

Caplow, Theodore, and Margaret Holmes Williamson. "Decoding Middletown's Easter Bunny: A Study in American Iconography," *Semiotica* 32 (1980): 221–32.

Carey, Diana, and Judy Large. *Festivals, Family, and Food*. Gloucestershire: Hawthorne Press, 1982.

Carlos, James, and Alan Gittelsohn. "Longitudinal Studies of the Natural History of Caries I: Eruption Patterns of the Permanent Teeth." *Journal of Dental Research* 44, no. 3 (1965): 509–14.

Carter, William, Bernard Butterworth, and Joseph Carter. *Ethnodentistry and Dental Folklore*. Kansas City, KS: Dental Folklore Books of Kansas City, 1987.

Cattell, James. "The Holiday Syndrome." *Psychoanalytic Review* 42 (1955): 39–43.

Caughey, John. *Imaginary Social Worlds*. Lincoln: University of Nebraska Press, 1984.

Cavendish, Richard, ed. *Man, Myth, and Magic: An Illustrated Encyclopedia of the Supernatural*. New York: Marshall Cavendish Corp., 1970.

Chalmers, Irena. *The Great Christmas Almanac*. New York: Viking Studio Books, 1988.

Chase, Mary. *Harvey*. New York: Dramatists Play Service, 1944.

Clark, Cindy Dell. "Putting Aside Adultcentrism: Child-Centered Ethnographic Research." Paper presented at the conference Reconceptualizing Research in Early Childhood Education, University of Wisconsin at Madison, October 1991.

Clark, Pauline. *The Return of the Twelves*. New York: Putnam's, 1962; reprint, New York: Dell Yearling Classic, 1986.

Coles, Robert. *The Spiritual Life of Children*. Boston: Houghton Mifflin, 1990.

Condry, John, and Freund, Sue. "Discriminating Real from Make-Believe on Television: A Developmental Study." Paper presented at the biannual meeting of the Society for Research in Child Development, Kansas City, Mo., 1989.

Coolidge, Frederick, and Duane Bracken. "The Loss of Teeth in Dreams: An Empirical Investigation." *Psychological Reports* 54 (1984): 931–35.

Coontz, Stephanie. *The Way We Never Were*. New York: Basic Books, 1992.

Corsaro, William A. *Friendship and Peer Culture in the Early Years*. Norwood, N.J.: Ablex Publishing, 1985.

Csikszentmihalyi, Mihaly, and Eugene Rochberg-Halton. *The Meaning of Things: Domestic Symbols and the Self*. Cambridge: Cambridge University Press, 1981.

Cutler, Blayne. "Here Comes Santa Claus (Again)." *American Demographics*, December 1989, 30–33.

Cummings, E. Mark, Carolyn Zahn-Waxler, and Marian Radke-Yarrow. "Developmental Changes in Children's Reactions to Anger in the Home." *Journal of Children Psychology and Psychiatry* 25 (1984): 63–74.

Darlington, H. S. "The Tooth-Losing Dream." *Psychoanalytic Review* 29 (1942): 71–79.

De Groot, Adrianus. *Saint Nicholas: A Psychoanalytic Study of His History and Myth*. The Hague: Mouton, 1965.

Denzin, Norman K. "The Politics of Childhood." In *Children and Their Caretakers,* ed. Norman Denzin, 1–25. New Brunswick, N.J.: Transaction Press, 1963.

Dixon, David J., and Harry L. Hom. "The Role of Fantasy Figures in the Regulation of Young Children's Behavior: Santa Claus, the Easter Bunny, and Donations." *Contemporary Educational Psychology* 9 (1984): 14–18.

Douglas, Mary. *Natural Symbols*. New York: Pantheon Books, 1982.

———. *Purity and Danger: An Analysis of the Concepts of Pollution and Taboo*. London: Ark Paperbacks, 1966; reprint 1985.

Ebon, Martin. *Saint Nicholas: Life and Legend*. New York: Harper & Row, 1975.

Eliade, Mircea. *Myth and Reality*. New York: Harper & Row, 1963.

————. *Patterns in Comparative Religion.* New York: New American Library, 1958.

————. *The Sacred and the Profane: The Nature of Religion.* New York: Harcourt Brace Jovanovich, 1959.

Elkind, David. *The Child's Reality: Three Developmental Themes.* Hillsdale, N.J.: Lawrence Erlbaum Associates, 1978.

Fine, Gary Alan. *With the Boys: Little League Baseball and Preadolescent Culture.* Chicago: University of Chicago Press, 1987.

Fine, Gary Alan, and Jay Mechling. "Minor Difficulties: Changing Children in the Late Twentieth Century." In *American at Century's End,* ed. Alan Wolfe, 58–78. Berkeley and Los Angeles: University of California Press, 1991.

Fischer, Eileen. "'Tis the Season to Be Jolly?: Tensions and Trends in Christmas Shopping." Paper presented at the annual meeting of the Association for Consumer Research, New Orleans, 1989.

Fischer, Eileen, and Stephen J. Arnold. "More Than a Labor of Love: Gender Roles and Christmas Gift Shopping." *Journal of Consumer Research* 17 (1990): 333–45.

Fisher-Thompson, Donna, Linda Polinski, Michele Eaton, and Kristin Heffernan. "Sex-Role Orientations of Children and Their Parents: Relationship to the Sex-Typing of Christmas Toys." Paper presented at the sixtieth anniversary meeting of the Society for Research in Child Development, New Orleans, March 1993.

Frazer, Sir James. *The Golden Bough: A Study of Magic and Religion.* 12 vols. London: Macmillan, 1915.

Freud, Sigmund. *The Interpretation of Dreams.* Translated by James Strachey. New York: Avon Books, 1965.

Gaskins, Suzanne, and John Lucy. "The Role of Children in the Production of Adult Culture: A Yucatec Case." Paper presented at the annual meeting of the American Ethnological Society, Philadelphia, 1987.

Gaskins, Suzanne, Peggy J. Miller, and William A. Corsaro. "Theoretical and Methodological Perspectives in the Interpretive Theory of Culture." *New Directions in Child Development* 58 (1992): 5–23.

Gitlin, Todd. "Television's Screens: Hegemony in Transition." In *American Media and Mass Culture: Left Perspectives,* ed. Donald Lazere, 240–65. Berkeley and Los Angeles: University of California Press, 1987.

Glassner, Barry. "Kid Society." *Urban Education* 11 (1976): 5–22.

Goodenough, Florence. *Anger in Young Children.* Minneapolis: University of Minnesota Press, 1931.

Granger, Byrd Howell. "Of the Teeth." *Journal of American Folklore* 74 (1982): 47–56.

Green, Edward. "Cargo Cults." In *Encyclopedia of Anthropology,* ed. David Hunter and Philip Whitten. New York: Harper & Row, 1976.

Greenberg, Bradley, and Byron Reeves. "Children and the Perceived Reality of Television." *Journal of Social Issues* 32 (1976): 86–97.

Hackett, Jo Ann, and John Huehnergard. "On Breaking Teeth." *Harvard Theological Review* 77, nos. 3–4) (1984): 259–75.

Haley, Mary. "Bidding a Sad Farewell to the Santa Claus of Early Childhood." *Chicago Parent,* January 1993, 4.

Hand, Wayland. "European Fairy Lore in the New World." *Folklore* 92, no. 2 (1981): 141–48.

Harris, Paul, and Robert Kavanaugh. "Young Children's Understanding of Pretense." *Monographs of the Society for Research in Child Development* 58, no. 1 (1993): 1–86.

Heller, David. *The Children's God.* Chicago: University of Chicago Press, 1986.

Hickey, Joseph V., William E. Thompson, and Donald L. Foster, "Becoming the Easter Bunny: Socialization into a Fantasy Role." *Journal of Contemporary Ethnography* 17, no. 1 (1988): 67–95.

Hirschman, Elizabeth, and Priscilla LaBarbara. "The Meaning of Christmas." In *Interpretive Consumer Research,* ed. Elizabeth Hirschman, 136–47. Provo, Utah: Association for Consumer Research, 1989.

Hole, Christina. *Easter and Its Customs.* New York: Barrows, 1961.

Imber-Black, Evan, Janine Roberts, and Richard Whiting. *Rituals in Families and Family Therapy.* New York: W. W. Norton, 1988.

Jalongo, Mary Renck. "Imaginary Companions in Children's Lives and Literature." *Childhood Education* 60 (1984): 166–71.

James, E. O. *Seasonal Feasts and Festivals.* New York: Barnes & Noble, 1961.

Jones, Charles. *Saint Nicholas of Myra, Bari, and Manhattan.* Chicago: University of Chicago Press, 1978.

Kakar, Sudir. *Shamans, Mystics, and Doctors.* Boston: Beacon Press, 1982.

Kanner, Leo. *Folklore of the Teeth.* New York: Macmillan, 1935.

———. "The Tooth as a Folkloristic Symbol." *Psychoanalytic Review* 15 (1928): 37–52.

Knapp, Mary, and Herbert Knapp. *One Potato, Two Potato: The Secret Education of American Children.* New York: W. W. Norton, 1976.

Knowlson, T. Sharper. *The Origin of Popular Superstitions and Customs.* London: T. Werner Laurie, 1930.

Lakoff, George, and Mark Johnson. *Metaphors We Live By.* Chicago: University of Chicago Press, 1980.

Layard, John. *The Lady of the Hare: Being a Study in the Healing Power of Dreams.* London: Faber and Faber, 1943.

Leach, Edmund. "Anthropological Aspects of Language: Animal Categories and Verbal Abuse." In *Reader in Comparative Religion,* ed. William Lessa and Evon Vogt, 153–66. New York: Harper & Row, 1964; reprint 1979.

Lévi-Strauss, Claude. "Where Does Father Christmas Come From?" *New Society* 19 (1963): 6–8.

Lincoln, Jackson Steward. *The Dream in Primitive Cultures.* London: Cresset Press, 1935; New York: Johnson Reprint Corp., 1970.

Lorand, Sandor. "On the Meaning of Losing Teeth in Dreams." *Psychoanalytic Quarterly* 17 (1948): 529–30.

Lorand, Sandor, and Sandor Feldman. "The Symbolism of Teeth in Dreams." *International Journal of Psychoanalysis* 36 (1955): 145–61.

Lord, Priscilla Sawyer, and Daniel Foley. *Easter Garland: A Vivid Tapestry of Customs, Traditions, Symbolism, Folklore, History, Legend, and Story.* Philadelphia: Chilton Books, 1963.

Lowry, Shirley Park. *Familiar Mysteries: The Truth in Myth.* New York: Oxford University Press, 1982.

Manosevitz, Martin, Norman Prentice, and Frances Wilson. "Individual and Family Correlates of Imaginary Companions in Preschool Children." *Developmental Psychology* 8, no. 1 (1973): 72–79.

Mead, Margaret. *Blackberry Winter.* New York: Pocket Books, 1972.

———. "An Investigation of the Thought of Primitive Children, with Special Reference to Animism." *Journal of the Royal Anthropological Institute* 62 (1932): 173–90.

Merton, Robert K., Marjorie Fiske, and Patricia L. Kendall. *The Focused Interview: A Manual of Problems and Procedures.* 2d ed. New York: Free Press, 1990.

Miller, Peggy, and Lisa Hoogstra. "How to Represent the Native Child's Point of View: Methodological Problems in Language Socialization." Paper presented at the annual meeting of the American Anthropological Association, Washington D.C., 1989.

Miller, Peggy, Lisa Hoogstra, Judith Mintz, Heidi Fung, and Kimberly Williams. "Troubles in the Garden and How They Get Resolved: A Young Child's Transformation of His Favorite Story." In *Memory and Affect in Development,* ed. Charles A. Nelson, 87–114. Hillsdale, N.J.: Lawrence Erlbaum Associates, 1993.

Milner, Marion. "D. W. Winnicott and the Two-way Journey." In *Between Reality and Fantasy: Transitional Objects and Phenomena,* ed. Simon Grolnick and Leonard Barkin, 37–42. New York: Jason Aronson, 1978.

Moore, Sally F., and Barbara Meyerhoff. *Secular Ritual.* Amsterdam: Van Gorcum, 1977.

Morison, Patricia, and Howard Gardner. "Dragons and Dinosaurs: The Child's Capacity to Differentiate Fantasy from Reality." *Child Development* 49 (1978): 642–48.

Morison, Patricia, Hope Kelly, and Howard Gardner. "Reasoning about the Realities of Television: A Developmental Study." *Journal of Broadcasting* 25 (1981): 229–41.

Morison, Patricia, Margaret McCarthy, and Howard Gardner. "Exploring the Realities of Television with Children." *Journal of Broadcasting* 23 (1979): 453–63.

Myers, Robert. *Celebrations: The Complete Book of American Holidays.* Garden City, N.Y.: Doubleday, 1972.

Newall, Venetia. *An Egg at Easter: A Folkloric Study.* Bloomington: Indiana University Press, 1971.

Nikola-Lisa, W. "The Cult of Peter Rabbit." Paper presented at a meeting of the Society for Popular Culture, Toronto, 1990.

Obeyesekere, Gananath. *Medusa's Hair: An Essay on Personal Symbols and Religious Experience*. Chicago: University of Chicago Press, 1981.

O'Connor, John, and Aaron Hoorwitz. "Imitative and Contagious Magic in the Therapeutic Use of Rituals with Children." In *Rituals in Families and Family Therapy*, ed. Evan Imber-Black, Janine Roberts, and Richard Whiting, 135–37. New York: W. W. Norton, 1988.

O'Flaherty, Wendy Doniger. *Dreams, Illusions, and Other Realities*. Chicago: University of Chicago Press, 1984.

———. "Inside and Outside the Mouth of God: The Boundary between Myth and Reality." *Daedalus* 109 (1980): 93–125.

———. *Other People's Myths*. New York: Macmillan, 1988.

Opie, Iona, and Peter Opie. *The Lore and Language of School Children*. London: Oxford University Press, 1959.

Ortner, Sherry. "Is Female to Male as Nature Is to Culture?" In *Women, Culture, and Society*, ed. Michelle Zimbalist Rosaldo and Louise Lamphere, 67–87. Stanford: Stanford University Press, 1974.

Oswalt, Wendell. "A Particular Pattern: Santa Claus." In *Understanding Our Culture: An Anthropological View*. New York: Holt, Rinehart & Winston, 1970.

Plath, David. "The Japanese Popular Christmas: Coping with Modernity." *Journal of American Folklore* 76 (1963): 309–17.

Pollock, George. "Temporal Anniversary Manifestations: Hour, Day, Holiday." *Psychoanalytic Quarterly* 40 (1971): 123–31.

Prentice, Norman, Martin Manosevitz, and Laura Hubbs. "Imaginary Figures of Early Childhood: Santa Claus, Easter Bunny, and the Tooth Fairy." *American Journal of Orthopsychiatry* 48 (1978): 618–28.

Preston, Samuel. "The Vanishing American Family: A Demographer's Perspective." *Penn Arts and Sciences*, Spring 1990, 8–10.

Proctor, James T. "Children's Reactions to Christmas." *Journal of the Oklahoma State Medical Association* 60 (1967): 653–59.

Pruyser, Paul. *The Play of the Imagination: Toward a Psychoanalysis of Culture*. New York: International Universities Press, 1983.

Rizzuto, Ana-Maria. *The Birth of the Living God: A Psychoanalytic Study*. Chicago: University of Chicago Press, 1979.

Robertson, Joyce. "A Mother's Observations of the Tonsillectomy of Her Four Year Old Daughter (with Commentary by Anna Freud)." *Psychoanalytic Study of the Child* 11 (1956): 410–33.

Rogoff, Barbara, Martha Sellers, Sergio Pirrotta, Nathan Fox, and Sheldon White. "Age of Assignment of Roles and Responsibilities in Children: A Cross-Cultural Survey." *Human Development* 18, no. 5 (1975): 353–69.

Scarlett, W. George, and Dennie Wolf. "When It's Only Make-Believe: The Construction of a Boundary between Fantasy and Reality in Storytelling." *New Directions for Child Development* 6 (1979): 29–40.

Scheff, T. J., *Catharsis in Healing, Ritual, and Drama.* Berkeley and Los Angeles: University of California Press, 1979.

Scheibe, Cynthia. "Developmental Differences in Children's Reasoning about Santa Claus and Other Fantasy Characters." Ph.D. diss., Cornell University, 1987.

———. "Learning the Categories of 'Real' and 'Make-Believe': A Developmental Study." Paper presented at the biannual meeting of the Society for Research in Child Development, Kansas City, Mo., 1989.

Schneck, Jerome. "Loss of Teeth in Dreams Symbolizing Fear of Aging." *Perceptual and Motor Skills* 24 (1967): 792.

———. "Total Loss of Teeth in Dreams." *American Journal of Psychiatry* 112 (1956): 939.

Schour, Isaac, and M. Massler. "The Development of Human Dentition." *Journal of the American Dental Association* 28 (1941): 1153–60.

Schwartz, Barry. "The Social Psychology of the Gift." *American Journal of Sociology* 73, no. 1 (1967): 1–11.

Sereno, Renzo. "Some Observations on the Santa Claus Custom." *Psychiatry* 14 (1951): 387–96.

Sherry, John. "Gift Giving in Anthropological Perspective." *Journal of Consumer Research* 10 (1983): 157–68.

Shweder, Richard. "How to Look at Medusa without Turning to Stone." *Contributions to Indian Sociology* 21 (1987): 37–55.

———. *Thinking through Cultures: Expeditions in Cultural Psychology.* Cambridge, Mass.: Harvard University Press, 1991.

Silvestro, John, "Second Dentition and School Readiness." *New York State Dental Journal* 43, no. 3 (1977): 155–58.

Sutton-Smith, Brian. *Toys as Culture.* New York: Gardner Press, 1986.

Tammivaara, Julie, and D. Scott Enright. "On Eliciting Information: Dialogues with Child Informants." *Anthropology and Education Quarterly* 17 (1986): 218–38.

Turner, Victor. *Celebration: Studies in Festivity and Ritual.* Washington, D.C.: Smithsonian Institution Press, 1982.

———. *The Forest of Symbols.* Ithaca: Cornell University Press, 1967.

———. *Ritual Process: Structure and Anti-structure.* Ithaca: Cornell University Press, 1969.

Van Allsburg, Chris. *The Polar Express.* Boston: Houghton Mifflin, 1985.

Van Gennep, Arnold. *The Rites of Passage.* Chicago: University of Chicago Press, 1960.

Verburge, Robert. "The Primacy of Metaphor in Development." *New Directions in Child Development* 6 (1979): 77–84.

Veyne, Paul. *Did the Greeks Believe in their Myths?* Chicago: University of Chicago Press, 1988.

Waida, Manabu. "Rabbits." In *The Encyclopedia of Religion,* ed. Mircea Eliade. New York: Macmillan, 1987.

Waksler, Frances. "Studying Children: Phenomenological Insights." *Human Studies* 9 (1986): 71–82.

Wallace, Anthony F. C. *Religion: An Anthropological View.* New York: Random House, 1966.

Warner, W. Lloyd. *The Family of God: A Symbolic Study of Christian Life in America.* New Haven: Yale University Press, 1961.

———. *The Living and the Dead: A Study of the Symbolic Life of Americans.* New Haven: Yale University Press, 1959.

Warshawski, Morrie. "Blessed Is the Tooth Fairy." *Parenting,* August 1987, 116.

Watkins, Mary. *Invisible Guests: The Development of Imaginal Dialogues.* Hillsdale, N.J.: Analytic Press, 1986.

Watts, Alan. *Easter: Its Story and Meaning.* London: Abelard-Schuman, 1950.

Webster, Hutton. "Rest Days: A Sociological Study." *University Studies* 11 (1911): 156–58.

Wells, Rosemary. "The Tooth Fairy." *Cal Magazine,* December 1979, 2–7.

———. "The Tooth Fairy, Part II." *Cal Magazine,* February 1980, 18–24.

———. "The Tooth Fairy, Part III." *Cal Magazine,* March 1980, 12–25.

———. "Tracking the Tooth Fairy: Blazing the Way." *Cal Magazine,* July 1983, 18–25.

———. "Tracking the Tooth Fairy: Conclusion." *Cal Magazine,* August 1983, 25–31.

———. "Tracking the Tooth Fairy: Finding the Trail." *Cal Magazine,* June 1983, 1–8.

Winner, Ellen. *The Point of Words: Children's Understanding of Metaphor and Irony.* Cambridge, Mass.: Harvard University Press, 1988.

Winnicott, D. W. *Playing and Reality.* London: Tavistock Publications, 1971.

———. "Transitional Objects and Transitional Phenomena." In *Collected Papers.* New York: Basic Books, 1951; reprint 1958.

Wreen, Michael. "Yes, Virginia, There Is a Santa Claus." *Informal Logic* 9, no. 1 (1987): 31–39.

Zaleski, Carol. *Otherworld Journeys: Accounts of Near-Death Experience in Medieval and Modern Times.* New York: Oxford University Press, 1987.

Zeitlin, Steven, Amy Kotkin, and Holly Cutting Baker. *A Celebration of American Family Folklore.* New York: Pantheon Books, 1982.

Zelizer, Viviana A. *Pricing the Priceless Child: The Changing Social Value of Children.* New York: Basic Books, 1985.

Zepp, Ira. *The New Religious Image of Urban America: The Shopping Mall as Ceremonial Center.* Westminster, Md.: Christian Classics, 1986.

Ziolkowski, Theodore. "The Telltale Teeth: Psychodontia to Sociodontia." *PMLA* 91 (1976): 9–22.

# Index

religion, 69, 110. *See* God; Resurrection; Jesus; Nativity
research method, 123–27
Resurrection, 61, 81, 90, 97
rice (wedding), 97
rite of passage: Easter Bunny as, 23, 109; giving up baby teeth as, 13–16; Santa Claus as, 23, 42, 109; seasonal (Christmas and Easter), 22–23, 60, 92, 97–98; stages of, 15
ritual: of bedtime, 21; benefits of, 118–19; child role in, 101–2, 105–6, 112, 119; of Christmas, 30–33; in contemporary America, 21; function of, 12, 99, 118–19; function of, in family, 31–33; of gift-giving, 28–30; and imaginal experience, 21; properties of, 83; and sacralization, 99–100; of Santa Claus, 30–31; of tooth loss, 9–10
Rochberg-Halton, Eugene, 87
Rockwell, Norman, 98
Roger Rabbit, 67–68
role-playing in child-centered research, 121–22
Roman Saturnalia, 23
Rudolph the Red-Nosed Reindeer, 27–28, 39, 57, 82, 92, 117; as child-driven myth, 104–5; identification of children with, 28; motif of, 105; offerings to, 105, 110; writing of, 28

sacred space, 69
sacredness: of commercial artifacts, 92–98; and paradox, 118
sacrifice, 33
sample for research, 124
Santa Claus: adult nostalgia for, 43–44; adult perspective on, 39–44, 93; adult role in myth, 46–47; as aligned with culture, 59, 61; belief in, 58; Catholic perspective, 56; child offerings to, 47–48; child perspective on, 50–52, 55; child role in myth, 46–48, 104–5; child versus adult perspective, 37; children's abstract understanding of, 58; and chimneys, 48; compared to the Eas-

ter Bunny, 62–64, 67–69, 81; connection to birth, 91; connection to God, 48–49, 53–58, 118; connection to Jesus, 61; emergence of disbelief in, 57–58; evidence of, 105; gift bag, 52–53, 93; and gift-giving, 45–48; and gift wrap, 52–53; as family ritual, 30–31; and hedonism, 93; history of, 24–27; letters to, 46–47; and materialism, 93–95; maternal perspective on, 47, 51; in mothers' field notes, 125–26; objections to, 2, 55–56, 113–18; offerings to, 47–48, 55; and omniscience, 46, 53–54; and the North Pole, 51; portrayals of, 26; as reinforcing childlike qualities, 41–44; research of, 121, 123–26; as rite of passage, 23, 42, 109; in shopping malls, 45–46, 63, 84, 92, 94–95, 102–3, 109, 114, 117; siblings' role in myth, 43; in social history, 27; as sociocentric ritual, 40–44; symbolism of, 49–51; and toys, 45–46; transcendent reality of, 53, 57–58, 109; as unreciprocated gift-giver, 29; visit of, 50–51
Satan, 116
Saturnus, 24
Saxon Yule feast, 23
Scheibe, Cynthia, 54–55
Schwartz, Barry, 46
Sears wish book, 92
second dentition: and dentists, 6; fear of, 9–10; maternal perspective on, 14; and other life changes, 14; physical discomfort of, 8–9; stages of, 15. *See also* tooth loss
secondary-process thought, 109
secrecy, 107; in the Christmas ritual, 40; in culture, 42; of the Easter Bunny, 68–70, 72; in eggs, 77; and gift-wrap, 52–53; of Santa Claus, 50–51; in the Tooth Fairy ritual, 17
separation as stage in rite of passage, 15
Sereno, Renzo, 30
Sesame Street, 85
shepherds, 24, 90
shopping mall: as centered space, 95;